Developing Student Leaders

ZONDERVAN/YOUTH SPECIALTIES BOOKS

Professional Resources

Called to Care
Developing Student Leaders
Feeding Your Forgotten Soul
Growing Up in America
Junior High Ministry
High School Ministry
How to Recruit and Train Volunteer Youth Workers (Previously released as Unsung Heroes)
The Ministry of Nurture
Organizing Your Youth Ministry
The Youth Minister's Survival Guide
Youth Ministry Nuts and Bolts

Discussion Starter Resources

Amazing Tension Getters
Get 'Em Talking
High School TalkSheets
Hot Talks
Junior High TalkSheets
Option Plays
Tension Getters
Tension Getters Two

Special Needs and Issues

The Complete Student Missions Handbook
Divorce Recovery for Teenagers
Ideas for Social Action
Intensive Care: Helping Teenagers in Crisis
Rock Talk
Teaching the Truth About Sex
Up Close and Personal: How to Build Community in Your Youth Group

Youth Ministry Programming

Adventure Games
Creative Programming Ideas for Junior High Ministry
Creative Socials and Special Events
Good Clean Fun
Good Clean Fun, Volume 2

Great Games for City Kids
Great Ideas for Small Youth Groups
Greatest Skits on Earth
Greatest Skits on Earth, Volume 2
Holiday Ideas for Youth Groups (Revised Edition)
Junior High Game Nights
On-Site: 40 On-Location Youth Programs
Play It! Great Games for Groups
Super Sketches for Youth Ministry
Teaching the Bible Creatively
The Youth Specialties Handbook for Great Camps and Retreats

4th-6th Grade Ministry

Attention Grabbers for 4th-6th Graders
Great Games for 4th-6th Graders
How to Survive Middle School
Incredible Stories
More Attention Grabbers for 4th-6th Graders
More Great Games for 4th-6th Graders
More Quick and Easy Activities for 4th-6th Graders
Quick and Easy Activities for 4th-6th Graders

Clip Art

ArtSource™ Volume 1—Fantastic Activities
ArtSource™ Volume 2—Borders, Symbols, Holidays, and Attention Getters
ArtSource™ Volume 3—Sports
ArtSource™ Volume 4—Phrases and Verses
ArtSource™ Volume 5—Amazing Oddities and Appalling Images
ArtSource™ Volume 6—Spiritual Topics
Youth Specialties Clip Art Book
Youth Specialties Clip Art Book, Volume 2

Developing Student Leaders

How to Motivate, Select, Train, and Empower Your Kids to Make a Difference

Ray Johnston

ZondervanPublishingHouse
Grand Rapids, Michigan
A Division of HarperCollins*Publishers*

Developing Student Leaders

Copyright © 1992 by Youth Specialties, Inc.

Youth Specialties Books, 1224 Greenfield Drive, El Cajon, California 92021, are published by Zondervan Publishing House, Grand Rapids, Michigan 49530

Library of Congress Cataloging-in-Publication Data

Johnston, Ray, 1952–
     Developing student leaders : how to motivate, select, train, and empower
your kids to make a difference / Ray Johnston.
          p. cm.
     Includes bibliographical references.
ISBN 0-310-54331-2
          1. Church work with teenagers. 2. Church youth workers.
     3. Christian leadership.   I. Title.
BV4447.J56 1992
259'.23—dc20   91-669
                                                                        CIP

Edited by Lory Floyd and Jeannette Larson
Designed and typography by JamisonBell Advertising and Design
Printed in the United States of America
92 93 94 95 96 97 98 99 / ML / 10 9 8 7 6 5 4 3

ABOUT THE YOUTHSOURCE™ PUBLISHING GROUP

YouthSource™ books, tapes, videos, and other resources pool the expertise of three of the finest youth ministry resource providers in the world:

- **Campus Life Books**—publishers of the award-winning *Campus Life* magazine, who for nearly fifty years have helped high schoolers live Christian lives.

- **Youth Specialties**—serving ministers to middle school, junior high, and high school youth for over twenty years through books, magazines, and training events such as the National Youth Workers Convention.

- **Zondervan Publishing House**—one of the oldest, largest, and most respected evangelical Christian publishers in the world.

CAMPUS LIFE	**YOUTH SPECIALTIES**	**ZONDERVAN**
465 Gundersen Dr.	1224 Greenfield Dr.	1415 Lake Dr. S.E.
Carol Stream, IL 60188	El Cajon, CA 92021	Grand Rapids, MI 49506
708/260-6200	619/440-2333	616/698-6900

Happy are those who dream dreams and are willing to pay the price to make them come true.

This book is affectionately dedicated to the three greatest influences in my life:

To my mom, who from day one believed in me and taught me to dream;

To my dad, who spent more time with his son than any other dad on the block;

To Carol, a wife whose authenticity, consistency, loyalty, and love continually remind me that dreams do come true.

Contents

Foreword

IN THE LATE 1970s my wife Cathy and I took eight high school students on a three-week "leadership" trip. We've never been as exhausted in our lives. We traveled 5,000 miles, counseled at a junior high camp, led Bible studies, experienced mission and service, backpacked, prayed together, played together, and I even remember a fight or two together. The funny thing was that all eight students ended up becoming our leadership core and, today, all eight students are in some form of ministry. They developed a lifestyle of servanthood almost accidently. I wish there had been a book like this back then. It would have been a positive force in youth ministry then, as it will be for this decade.

This is the book and the subject for good, positive, life-changing youth ministry in the 1990s. Youth ministry is changing, and I think for the better. In my opinion, the most important changes are in the area of developing student leadership. For several years we talked about student leadership and yet, frankly, we did very little to cultivate leadership in our youth ministry programs. We can no longer depend on entertainment, rallies, or fun and games to keep kids serious about their Christian commitment. The kids who are involved in leadership today are the ones who will be staying in the church; taking on adult leadership positions; and serving the Lord through full-time ministry.

This subject is the message of the nineties and my friend, Ray Johnston, is the best person in the world to present this important topic. Ray Johnston, the theorist, has provided an outstanding model for developing student leaders. His theory is cutting-edge youth ministry with real substance. Ray Johnston, the practitioner, is readable and very practical—and you will find yourself implementing his ideas immediately. Ray's years of hands-on youth work in the church, combined with his teaching skills make Developing Student Leaders a must read.

I believe in Ray Johnson and in his message. He is an "impactor" for impactors. Ray is a leader, a model, and one of the best communicators in the country. Through these pages Ray gives us some of the finest youth ministry material ever written. I hope he will be your mentor as you implement these important principles.

Yours in Christ,
Jim Burns
President, National Institute of Youth Ministry

Acknowledgments

SPECIAL THANKS TO GARY COPELAND AND JOHN BRAY—two senior pastors whose support, encouragement, and ability to let us try almost anything enabled our leadership program more than they will ever realize.

I would like to express my deep appreciation to the following student leaders and staff members who during our seven years together at Marin Covenant Church served faithfully, lived authentically, and put up with all kinds of experiments in our efforts to develop leaders who would make a long-term impact. I thank God upon all my remembrance of you!

Amy Adams
Mimi Agers
Jon Aguirre
Caralee Albarian
Kim Ammann
DeeDee Cundall Anderson
Ginger and Jesse Apperson
Sandy Aradi
Kirsten, Michelle, and Liesl Arensmeier
Jon Aunger
Cole and Lawson Bader
Kerry and Steve Barthel
Angie Paraskos Bazalgette
Holly Gilbreath Bell
Barbie Betic
Gary Black, Jr.
Sean Blomquist
Kirsten Blomquist
Larry and Susanna Boeck
Libby Bray

Claudia Breuer
Rob Bridges
Emily Budge
Sue Burroni
Lisa and Debbie Bush
Jeremy Chaffin
Bill Chiaravalle
Dave Collins
Tony Collins
Lisa Copeland
Shawn Coppin
John Cowley
Kim Coyle
Wendy Crawford
Jeanne Cuthbert
Kirsten Daily
Abigail and Rebekah Davis
Allison and Peter de Laveaga
JoAnn and Sandy Deasy
Amy and Lisa Dobyns
J. P. Dorn
Jenny Dressel
Randy Edens

John Eldridge
Rosanne Faul
John Faymost
Gary Gaddini
Eileen Gilmore
Lynn Gordon
Alison Gourlay
Paul Gray
Lydia and Laura Greenfield
Dave Hakim
Anna-Lisa Mattson Helmy
Anne Herrmann
Mark and Joe Heuvelhorst
Laurie and Gage Houser
Carol Johnston
Karen Jordan
Kelly Jordan
Jana Jung
Eric Kaiser
Dave Keane
Mary Kennaugh

Ken and Bob Kennedy
Aliesha Gray Kingsman
Karen and Rick Klug
Mark and Greg Krieger
John Lagoy
Karen Lancaster
Katie Lang
Patty Bohan Lauterjung
Amy Lewis
Kathy Putnam Loomis
Jon Lovins
Dave and Jenny Mahar
Mike Manookian
Trish Marino
Dave Mason
Kristine and Donna Matisek
Jennifer Michaels
Elisa and Renata Montiel
Neil Moyer
Julie Neil
Dan and Ginny Nichols
Craig Nierman
Maria Nissen
John and Elizabeth O'Neal

Stacey Padrick
Heather Paraskos
Michelle Parsley
Joe and Kerry Pere
Greg and Leslie Peterson
Laura Pinkney
Jamene Pinnow
Gordon and Elizabeth Pipes
Kent Place
Steve Quartly
Nic Quinzon
Suzy and Tom Qvistgaard
Wes, Becca, and Matt Reed
Doug Richardson
MaryBeth Richardson
Doug Robinson
Michelle Rodrigues
Diana Rose-Zweng
Bob and Ron Sage
Scott and Sally Shaull
Teresa Sherlock
Mike and Mary Shimmin

Marilyn Siems
Kelly Stanley
Mike Sturdt
Allison and Jason Swider
Jeff Taylor
Hugo Tejada
Becca Thoms
Jennifer Touchstone
Kerri Trexler
Tim Vincent
Jerry and Cathi VonSchimmelmann
Dan and Rob Wade
Barbara Walker
Nancy Warfield-Perkins
Anna, Maria, and Mike Wecker
Greg and Mari West
Wendy Williams
Matt Wilson
Teresa Wilson-Watts
Andrew Wodecki
Mike Wold
Marci Ziebel

Foundations:
The Brave, the Few,
the Student Leaders

Why Develop Student Leaders?

I SAT LISTENING IN AMAZEMENT as a longtime friend of mine described his feelings of frustration and burnout and his desire to leave his youth ministry. For the average youth worker in a typical church, those feelings usually come with the territory, but this situation was far from average.

He had a state-of-the-art youth ministry most of us would envy. He was working in a huge church with all of the benefits: up-to-date equipment, a sizeable budget, awesome resources, a great salary (a youth ministry miracle), a full-time secretary, tremendous support from the church family, and even the use of a new bus that, unlike most church buses, didn't break down every time he used it.

His busy program included several world-class mission trips, dazzling outreach events, a growing small group ministry, a well-staffed Sunday school, and a thriving weekly outreach program that drew hundreds of students. In short, he was running a youth ministry most of us would love to take over.

That may have been precisely the problem. He was running the program! As I listened to him describe feelings of burnout, he admitted that his youth ministry had become a one-man show. He hadn't included the development of student leadership anywhere in his program and, as a result, all of the responsibilities lay squarely on his shoulders. He had to be at every meeting, set up every room, plan every event, lead every song, and give every talk. He had not developed any student leaders whom he could trust with significant responsibility. Later that year, both the kids and the parents were disappointed when he left the church and moved out of town.

That conversation was an eye-opener for me, and it confirmed one of the key lessons I have learned in the last fifteen years of youth ministry. *For eliminating youth worker burnout, turning around apathetic, uninvolved kids, and building long-term success in youth ministry, nothing equals a student leadership development program.*

Someone said there are three types of people in the world—those who watch what happens, those who make things happen, and those who scratch their heads and wonder what in the world is happening.

13

The ability to make things happen is the gift of leadership; developing that gift in students is critical for their futures, as well as for our own sanity.

How do you define leadership? Leadership in its truest sense is influence. Developing leaders is the art of enabling others to make things happen. In thinking about the functions of leadership, it is helpful to think of three basic areas.

First, **organizational leaders** are individuals who influence a group or organization by planning, goal setting, and directing. All organizations, youth ministries included, have groups of people who set the agenda and determine the goals and direction. Individuals who make things happen at this level are the organizational leaders. These leaders are usually in positions of overseeing the group or organization. All too often students have little input or responsibility at this level.

Personal leaders are individuals involved in making things happen. These people, many of whom are not typical "natural leaders" with tremendous up-front skills, tend to lead by influencing people individually or in groups rather than organizationally. Although many would never view themselves as leaders, they are often involved in personal evangelism, counseling, or discipling relationships that have a great influence on those with whom they work.

Program leaders are the people who plan and lead the programs of the organization. In a typical youth ministry, there is a wide array of programs requiring an even wider variety of gifted people to successfully pull them off. Many times students come to their own youth groups to watch the adults lead a large majority of the programs.

I learned years ago that leadership involvement at any of these three levels can be a very growth producing experience. When I was a relatively new Christian and was just beginning college, I was asked to lead a Bible study for a group of high school guys. My exposure to the Bible up until that time was so new that I could empathize with the student in our group who wondered aloud if Joan of Arc was Noah's wife. Because of my limited knowledge, it was everything I could do just to stay one step ahead of the hounds. As I look back (and laugh about) that first attempt at leading a Bible study program, I recognize that experience as a turning point in my young Christian life. As a result of the opportunity to lead a program, I gained a much deeper appreciation for the Scriptures. I also learned to lead as I stumbled through the successes and failures of leading a program for the first time.

Many youth ministers have yet to discover that the most effective way to change the lives of students is to get them involved in service and leadership. We often fail to realize that teenagers can be challenged and trained to handle key organizational, personal, and program leadership responsibilities. This failure leads to overworked, exhausted youth workers who, like my friend, burn out after two short years in even the best of situations.

This book will suggest a shift in the way we design our youth programs. Most youth ministries go in one of two directions—they either *entertain* students or they *equip* students. Each route leads to a different destination. The results are dramatic. When we major in *entertaining* students, we will most likely produce *spectators*. If we take on the challenge of *equipping* students for leadership, we will produce *servant leaders*.

Three convictions lead me to believe that equipping students for leadership ought to be top priority for youth ministry.

Leadership development is the only known antidote for apathy. It doesn't take the intelligence of a rocket scientist to see that our kids are being shaped by a culture that is increasingly self-absorbed and apathetic.

• A university professor recently described the incoming freshman class by saying, "They remind me of passengers on the *Titanic*. They know the ship is going down, but all they want are first-class seats as it sinks."

• In a recent letter to *TV Guide*, a concerned writer asked, "In the event of a nuclear war, could the electromagnetic impulses from exploding bombs destroy my videotapes?"

• During the Persian Gulf war, a college student was asked about his plans for the night. He replied, "I'm going back to my room to make some popcorn, sit on the couch, and watch the war."

We live in a spectator society. Recently, while teaching on this subject, I asked the class, "How would you define apathy?" One response was immediate: "Who cares?" That phrase sounds familiar because, as I look back on past youth ministry experiences, I realize I spent years producing apathetic students. It wasn't intentional. I didn't have a five-step plan for producing apathy. I just ignored a fundamental leadership principle: People get excited and support what *they* create and lead!

Every teacher, parent, or youth worker has a few kids who drive them crazy. One of mine was a student named John. When John was a high school senior he met every high school status requirement: good looks, athletic ability, a great car, a bright future, and an invitation to every party. He also thought he was too cool for life—too cool for the church, for his parents, for his younger brother, and probably for God himself. I think the guy was born with sunglasses on. I will never know why he signed up to be a leader in our mission trip to Mexico (he probably thought it was cool), but as I watched him in ministry that week, I saw a high school student transformed right before my eyes. John gave his life to Christ, joined our student leadership team, and never recovered from the experience. He is now a youth pastor at a church in California and his "too cool for life" kids are probably driving him nuts. I'm loving every minute of it! Involvement in leadership transformed John's apathetic indifference to concerned involvement.

John Howard says it best.

> Having spent a career trying to understand and help young people, I am convinced that the one primary cause of the tragic self-destruction of so many of our youth is that they do not know the work and satisfaction of living for something larger than themselves. The human psyche cannot stand up against moral neutrality. If nothing is truly good, right, and worth striving and sacrificing for, life is meaningless and no course of action can build a sense of one's own self-worth. Without large goals, life is barren, life is a burden.[1]

Because the Christian church is always one generation away from extinction, it is in constant need of a new generation of Christian leaders. The students who fill that need will be the ones we help overcome indifference by enabling them to discover the call of God today!

One New Testament professor hit the nail on the head when he declared that, "In my estimation, the greatest threat to Christianity is not communism, not atheism, and not cultism. . . . In my estimation, the greatest threat to Christianity is Christians who are trying to sneak into heaven incognito, without ever sharing their faith or becoming involved."[2] The antidote for apathy is involvement in leadership.

Leadership development is essential for long-term effectiveness in youth ministry. I had an experience several summers ago that became a turning point in the way I approached youth ministry.

I had spent years in youth ministry designing, planning, and promoting outreach events with absolute confidence that the kids in our youth group would march onto their campuses and bring huge numbers of their friends to the events. In terms of effectiveness, most of the time I was lucky if our own kids showed up. I was midway through an ineffective summer planning meeting when I dropped the idea of a Burger Bash (a-free-hamburger-bring-your-starving-friends-outreach-event) on our group of twelve student leaders—with the complete confidence that they would love the idea. I finished the pitch and waited for their enthusiastic responses. They were underwhelmed. Reactions varied from, "I don't think it will work," to "No way would I bring my friends to that." My response was, "Well, what do you think will work, a Quiche Bash?" At this, the dead meeting took an amazing turn. One shy student spoke up and said, "Wait a minute. Why don't we try the event with pizza?" The whole group (ignoring my previous burger idea) thought it was a great idea! For the next twenty minutes, apathy was replaced by excited conversation as they planned the world's first Pizza Bash. They were on the edges of their chairs as they talked about planning and promoting the event and guessed how many free pizzas they might get because Domino's couldn't deliver seventy-five pizzas on thirty minutes notice. As they decided on the program, music, sports, games, and publicity (5,000 business cards saying Pizza Bash), I realized that three things had happened:

1. Ownership for the event had shifted from leader to students. The program and publicity were now *their* ideas; the reins of leadership were now in the hands of the students.

2. Ownership led to support and excitement for the program. Apathy and boredom were ancient history. The students were fired up, excited about their program and ideas, and ready to work to pull it off. I no longer had to push them—they were ready to run me over as they stampeded toward the event.

3. Support and excitement produced dramatic results. The night of the event arrived and so did I, with some reservations. I was wondering how I was going to explain the expense of seventy-five pizzas for a grand total of twelve kids. Our leaders arrived first, and I was soon converted after 411 of their friends arrived. It was by far our largest high school event and became a successful annual activity. Our effectiveness in reaching teenagers increased dramatically the minute the students held the reins of leadership. Whether or not a youth ministry experiences long-term growth and effectiveness often depends entirely on time invested in developing and equipping student leaders.

Leadership development is critical because your own survival depends on it. Most "omni-competent" youth workers are busy. Too busy. Developing teams of student leaders will lead to a longer, happier, and healthier career in youth ministry. It may even give you some valuable extra time for your family.

Four years ago I was looking ahead on our youth ministry calendar when Carol and I discovered that the due date for our first child was right in the middle of our yearly week-long mission trip to Mexico. I quickly realized that I had three options. One, I could cancel the trip and have eighty-five upset teenage missionaries camping on my front lawn. Two, I could go on the trip and end up permanently living in a tent on that same lawn. Three, I could train a group of student leaders who, with our adult volunteers, would lead the trip without me.

This event was a great lesson in humility. We trained the student leaders and off they went to Mexico. It was amazing—they made it to Mexico, had a great week of ministry, and returned safely, all without the benefit of my indispensable presence. One kid said it was the finest mission trip he had experienced. They enjoyed their mission trip, and I enjoyed being home for the birth of our first son, Mark.

As I talked with the friend that I mentioned at the start of this chapter, I realized that in the midst of his running a well-rounded youth ministry program he may have missed his most valuable resource: the students in his youth group. Too often they go undiscovered and undeveloped. We talk about looking for volunteers, but we don't have to look for kids—they are right there. The youth worker who dares to develop the kids' abilities for leadership will find students moving from apathy to involvement, will discover effectiveness in youth ministry, and may begin working smarter, not harder. Developing student leaders is not an option. It is essential for long-term growth and health.

Endnotes

1. John A. Howard, *In Touch Newsletter* 3, no. 1 (September 1990): 2.
2. James Stewart, *In Touch Newsletter* 3, no. 1 (September 1990): 1.

Benefits of Developing Student Leaders

Important
*

BEFORE JAMES GARFIELD BECAME PRESIDENT of the United States, he was president of Hiram College. One day a father asked him about the curriculum. Garfield began to list the courses the son would have to take. The man, obviously irritated, interrupted and said, "Mr. Garfield, that is far too much work for the degree he will get. Couldn't you make it easier?" "Yes, I suppose I could," replied Garfield. "But I am reminded that when God wants to build a tall, strong oak tree, he takes a hundred years. But he only takes three months to make a squash. What do you want your son to be, an oak tree or a squash?"[1]

That is a pertinent question in the spiritual realm as well. Leadership development is tough work and the curriculum is demanding, but involvement in leadership has some specific "oak-tree-like" benefits for your students, the whole church, and you.

Involvement in leadership helps students develop commitment and dedication. In his book *Revolution Now*, Bill Bright includes the following quote from a Communist student who is breaking his engagement with his fiancee. Notice the commitment and dedication that comes from involvement in leadership.

> We Communists have a high casualty rate. We are the ones who get shot and hung and ridiculed and fired from our jobs and in every other way made as uncomfortable as possible. A certain percentage of us get killed or imprisoned. We live in virtual poverty. We turn back to the party every penny we make above what is absolutely necessary to keep us alive. We Communists do not have the time or the money for many movies, or concerts, or T-bone steaks, or decent homes, or new cars. We have been described as fanatics. We are fanatics. Our lives are dominated by one great overshadowing factor: The struggle for world communism. We Communists have a philos-

ophy of life which no amount of money can buy. We have a cause to fight for, a definite purpose in life. We subordinate our petty personal selves into great movement of humanity; and if our personal lives seem hard or our egos appear to suffer through subordination to the party then we are adequately compensated by the thought that each of us in his small way is contributing to something new and true and better for mankind. There is one thing in which I am in dead earnest about, and that is the Communist cause. It is my life, my business, my religion, my hobby, my sweetheart, my wife, and my mistress, my breath and meat. I work at it in the daytime and dream of it at night. Its hold on me grows, not lessens as time goes on; therefore, I cannot carry on a friendship, a love affair, or even a conversation without relating it to this force which both drives and guides my life. I evaluate people, books, ideas, and actions according to how they affect the Communist cause, and by their attitude toward it. I've already been in jail because of my ideals, and if necessary, I'm ready to go before a firing squad.[2]

Bright is amazed that Christians, who above all people ought to believe in the capability of people to make an impact, invest so little time developing their God-given gifts for leadership. Involvement in leadership develops character and commitment.

Involvement in leadership helps students develop confidence and self-esteem. Contemporary adolescents have grown up in a society that majors in tearing them down. The average student feels like everyone is on his or her back and no one is on his or her side. Typical of the constant feedback given to the average teenager are the words written in the annual of a good friend of mine.

> God created rivers,
> God created lakes,
> God created you, Bob,
> Everyone makes mistakes.

Merton Strommen in *Five Cries of Youth*[3] states that the number one cry of teenagers is the cry of self-hatred. Surveys back this up. Of American teenagers, 80 percent don't like the way they look and the other 20 percent probably lied on the survey.[4] Many teenagers feel that if being ugly was a crime, they'd be in jail. The average campus in America is a self-image war zone and an overwhelming number of the students are casualties. To make matters worse, the average church often compounds the problem. When the students are not leading the ministry, they come away from our programs impressed with *us*: *our* speaking abilities, *our* song leading, *our* sense of humor, *our* knowledge of Scripture, *our* brand-new Youth Specialties fluorescent flannelgraph, and so on. All of which makes *us* feel great but does nothing to build the self-esteem and confidence so necessary to the growth and development of teenagers.

The building of confidence and high levels of self-esteem are critical for the long-term development of healthy teenagers. Studies show that adolescents with low self-esteem are more susceptible to peer pressure, are more likely to engage in the high-risk behaviors of alcohol and drug abuse, are more often suicidal, and are more likely to seek acceptance through sexual experimentation.

Getting students involved at the leadership level of the youth ministry has tremendous benefits in the area of self-esteem. In his book *The Antecedents of Self-Esteem*, Stanley Coopersmith suggests four essential components to a healthy self-image: significance, competence, power, and virtue.[5] Involvement in leadership gives kids a sense that they are making a difference (significance); training for leadership develops skills (competence); holding responsibility for leadership lets students feel they are making the major decisions (power); and handling leadership responsibility develops character (virtue).

Involvement in leadership enables students to discover the ability to make decisions and keep commitments. Let's face it—the ability to make decisions is a vital skill, and this generation of teenagers is not known for its qualities of decision making and commitment. I realized this during my first couple of years in youth ministry. I would ask student after student about future plans, for the weekend or for anything else, and was sure to be answered by the phrase, "I don't know." The eminent theologian Dr. Seuss may have been describing the average indecisive adolescent when he penned the following little known poem:

THE ZODE

Did I ever tell you about the young Zode?
Who came to two signs at the fork in the road,
One said to Place one, and the other, Place two.
So the Zode had to make up his mind what to do.
Well . . . the Zode scratched his head, and his chin and his pants.

And he said to himself, "I'll be taking a chance
If I go to Place one. Now, that place may be hot!
And so, how do I know if I'll like it or not?
On the other hand though, I'll be sort of a fool
If I go to Place two and I find it too cool
In *that* case I may catch a chill and turn blue!
So, maybe Place one is the best, not Place two
But then again, what if Place one is too high?
I may catch a terrible earache and die!
So Place two may be best! On the other hand though . . .
What might happen to me if Place two is too low?
I might get some very strange pain in my toe!
So Place one may be best." And he started to go.
Then he stopped, and he said, "On the other hand though . . .
On the other hand . . . other hand . . . other hand though. . . ."
And for 36 hours and a ½ that poor Zode
Made starts and made stops at the fork in the road.
Saying, "Don't take a chance. No! You may not be right."
Then he got an idea that was wonderfully bright!
"Play safe!" cried the Zode. "I'll play safe! I'm no dunce!
I'll simply start out for both places at once!"
And that's how the Zode who would not take a chance
Got to no place at all with a split in his pants.[6]

Like the guy in the story, there are a lot of teenagers in the world without direction because of their inability to make decisions and keep commitments.

In leadership, the demand for decisions comes with the territory. Leaders are forced to make decisions. Student leaders have the opportunity to be involved in setting goals and objectives, determining direction, setting the content for the education classes, picking the meeting times, choosing the retreat sites, picking the potential volunteers, setting the rules, and planning the programs. Decision making is a vital skill that is best developed by practice. Involvement in leadership provides that opportunity.

Involvement in leadership leads to student ownership and support of the youth ministry. Probably the most important principle in management states that people support what *they* create. Decision-making responsibility leads to ownership, which usually leads to support and success.

It was going to be great. I was two months into my new youth ministry at Marin Covenant Church, and I had gathered a group of students to plan a retreat designed to attract their friends. Because no one knows what will interest and attract a high school student like another high school student, I gave the teenagers the assignment to come up with a retreat that their friends would jump at the chance to attend. I gave them fifteen minutes and left the room. When I came back, I wished I hadn't returned. They had decided on a snow skiing trip. As they described the retreat, I realized that every person in the room was excited—except me. They had managed to pick a retreat with the one sport I had never tried. I had heard that there is no way to look cool while learning to ski (a fact that I personally confirmed), and the thought of looking like a complete fool in front of my youth group at our first retreat really didn't turn me on. Nevertheless, the decision was theirs and it was final. The results were dramatic. Because of their ownership of the event, they were committed to bringing their friends. They had confidence in the event because it was their idea. It was the largest retreat in the church's history. Several of their friends made Christian commitments, and the group came back with great videos of a youth pastor laying in the snow, which they used as a promotional video for the next year's ski retreat. Giving students responsibility for leadership and decision making leads to great results. It may be a little uncomfortable, but it's definitely worth every risk.

Involvement in leadership teaches kids that God wants to build and use their gifts and abilities. Students are largely devoid of purpose, direction, or a sense of mission. Stephen Glenn claims that this generation of teenagers is the first to grow up and discover that they are completely unnecessary.[7] David Elkind describes this generation with the phrase, "All grown up and no place to go."[8] Many of today's teenagers are graduating to discover they are highly equipped to be perfectly useless. Involvement in leadership is the key to helping students get on a road to a lifetime of Christian service.

At first, thirty-five of our high school students were disappointed. It was Sunday morning and we had just arrived at the church in Mexico that was to serve as our headquarters for a week of ministry. The students had spent three months planning, preparing, and praying that God would use them on this trip. Upon arriving at the small, rural village, it was obvious that something was wrong. The church where we were going to serve had been badly burned; the roof had caved in and now only the four walls remained. We arrived as a weary, weather-beaten Mexican pastor and nine parishioners were midway through their Sunday service. We filed into the back of the burned-out church, greeted only by the amazed stares of the nine parishioners. At the end of a hymn, the pastor, probably figuring this was more than just a good response to "Visitor Sunday," stopped the service. He walked back and said, "Que pasa?" which I think meant, "What in the world are you yuppies doing here?" It turned out they had not been contacted by the Mission Board and had no idea we were coming. There was a long silence until one of the student leaders explained that we were Christians and were here to serve. I will never forget what followed. The pastor, uncharacteristically choked up, said, "They (the villagers) burned down our church six months ago. We've been praying that God would send help but had given up hope of help ever coming!" Our kids were stunned silent (for the first time in history) because, although they had heard a million times that God desired to use their lives, they were now experiencing it for the first time. During a team meeting later, one student declared in amazement, "We are an answer to prayer!" He was right on target. Back home they often were viewed by others and occasionally themselves as problems. But the minute we motivate and involve students in the process of leadership, they become the answer to someone's prayer.

The youth ministry as a whole is strengthened by the development of student leadership. The benefits of a core of committed student leaders may be one of the greatest gifts that a youth pastor can give to the church. Youth ministries are legendary for starting fast and dropping even faster. Students get excited about a new program and it takes off and lasts for a whole month. As student leaders learn the value of commitment for the long haul, the youth ministry will develop longer staying power because it is based on a broadened base of leadership.

The youth ministry will also be able to expand what it attempts to accomplish. Rest home ministries, mission trips, socials, birthday celebrations, and student newspapers take time and energy and few youth pastors can handle that type of load. A number of wonderful ministries our church loved were planned, staffed, and run by high school students. They would never have taken place without student involvement.

The youth ministry will experience growth. Nature teaches us a fundamental principle: Where there is life, there is growth. While most of us are uncomfortable using numerical growth as a measure of success, it sure beats the opposite. The ownership students experience as they are involved in leadership generates enthusiasm, and turned-on kids are like magnets to their friends. Our youth ministry only began to grow numerically after our leadership team solidified.

The youth ministry will experience a deeper level of care and nurture. Kids can be trained to take the lead in caring for one another. Each year we had several students involved in a Big Brother/Big Sister program. They gave time to younger students, many of whom were struggling just to find one friend as they began high school. Solid relationships formed as our older students began to give leadership to some of our younger students.

When students are involved in leadership, we will do a better job of proclaiming the Gospel. Kids listen to kids. I spoke last year at an event in Canada called Youthquake. What an intimidating event! It's Canada's largest youth event: 4,000 teenagers, the Canadian Women's Olympic Volleyball Team, big name bands, and so on. During one of the meetings, a very nervous sophomore boy stepped up to the microphone to talk about his faith in Christ. As he struggled to speak, you could have heard a pin drop. He kept 4,000 students riveted as he described the impact that Christ had in his life. When he finished he was greeted with a thunderous standing ovation. It left the rest of us who were speaking wishing that we were teenagers. Kids listen best to other kids. For the Gospel to be effectively presented in youth ministry, it needs to be presented by teenagers.

The church's other ministries benefit from students trained in leadership. As the student leaders grow, the church as a whole benefits. A strong youth ministry is a church growth magnet. A recent survey indicated that a strong youth ministry is the number two factor in whether or not a church grows. People, especially parents of teenagers, often choose a church because it ministers to their kids. I have friends who have told me they will tolerate almost anything in a church if their kids are growing spiritually.

Students involved in leadership are able to contribute to the ministry of the whole church. As our students began to discover their gifts and abilities, they got involved in teaching Sunday school and helping with the Sunday morning service. Our summer Vacation Bible School was staffed to a great degree by high school and junior high students.

A youth ministry with student leadership will enable the church to hang onto its kids. A national survey was taken to discover the major causes for the rejection of religion by teenagers.[9] Teenagers who had chosen to leave their churches were asked their reasons for the exit. As I read the study, I expected the responses to be peer pressure, drugs, sex, hypocrisy, and bad retreat food. The number one answer was startling. The survey revealed that the teenagers' most often stated reason for rejection of religious faith was "lack of meaningful involvement in the life of the church." Most teenagers are convinced that there is little place for them in the church and even less in the field of leadership. Teenagers will take our churches seriously when they know that the church is taking them seriously. Positive faith is best developed in the context of commitment, community, and involvement; those three essentials thrive in the context of building leadership teams.

The youth pastor benefits from student involvement in leadership. The church and the kids did grow as a result of student leadership involvement, but probably the one who derived the greatest benefit was me. I loved the fun and enjoyment of working with committed kids. Let's be honest—a lot of youth ministry, especially the big events, is just plain hard work. Unlike a lot of events that left me drained and wondering where I had put that resignation letter, time with motivated kids where they were planning and doing the work was invigorating. If you are spending all of your time working with the whole group and are enjoying it less, it may not be time to get out of ministry—it may be time to shift gears and begin working with kids you can develop.

Working with student leaders kept me on my toes spiritually. After one of our student leadership meetings, I headed off to play in a church basketball league. Several of the guys came with me and were in the stands supporting and laughing at their local youth pastor. On one particularly bad call, I was in the midst of giving the referee a piece of my mind (which, frankly, I couldn't afford to lose) when one of the guys caught my eye and gave me that "try to be an example for me" look. I immediately shut up and went back to the game. When we disciple leadership, it has a way of keeping us on our toes spiritually.

Working with student leaders gave me hope. Knowing that I was developing leaders continually reignited my passion for youth ministry. It happens to every youth pastor at some point in youth ministry—I call it the "esoteric awareness flash." It usually happens for the first time in the midst of a game with junior highers. We suddenly look around and say, "Hey, I'm thirty years old and I'm still playing the egg-in-the-armpit relay with kids." That is followed by the "My friends are doctors and lawyers and I'm still playing games with their kids" syndrome. In moments like these, my sense that all kids, no matter what stage of their growth and development, were future candidates for significant leadership kept me going. If all I'm doing is running games to entertain kids, then let's go sell Amway. But if those young men and women are future leaders who just may make significant contributions, then let's stay with it.

Developing student leaders also made me more effective. Because I stopped thinking I had to work with every kid and personally handle every responsibility, I had more time and energy to give to higher priorities. Student leaders will enable us to make better use of our time and energy. Continually operating outside of the areas of our strengths usually leads to personal frustration and organizational ineffectiveness. One of my professors in seminary jarred me when he stated, "If you want to have an exciting life, find out what your spiritual gifts are and build your whole life around them." Church management experts tell us that most of us spend up to 90 percent of our time operating in the areas of our weaknesses or doing that which will not bring results. My student leadership teams handled huge amounts of responsibilities, which freed me to operate in areas for which I am trained. In my last four years at Marin Covenant, I never had to set up or take down a room. That was taken care of by the "Scenic Engineering Team," a group of students who handled that responsibility.

Working with student leaders has given me the gift of some very special lifelong friendships. I recently received a long distance call from two of my favorite people, Mark and Kim. Now graduating from college, they had been on our student leadership team while they were in high school. As we talked, they excitedly informed my wife and me of their engagement and asked if I would perform the wedding. What an honor! As I later reflected on the continuing friendship, I realized that a bond, which may last a lifetime, is often formed when students and youth workers work side by side.

When we involve teenagers the benefits are unbelievable. They become the stars. They discover that they have gifts and abilities. They discover that they are capable. They discover that you trust them with significant responsibility. They discover that they are taken seriously. They discover that they can fail and survive it. They discover that God can use them. They discover that you value them and want to use them. They become a resource for the entire church, and they may end up impacting your life more than you have impacted theirs.

Endnotes

1. James A. Garfield, as quoted in Gary Inrig, *Hearts of Iron, Feet of Clay* (Chicago: Moody Press, 1979), 95.

2. Bill Bright, *Revolution Now* (San Bernardino, Calif.: Campus Crusade for Christ, 1969), 186-87.

3. Merton Strommen, *Five Cries of Youth* (New York: Harper and Row, 1974), 12.

4. Jim Burns, *Surviving Adolescence* (Waco, Tex.: Word, 1990), 34.

5. Stanley Coopersmith, *The Antecedents of Self-Esteem* (Palo Alto, Calif.: Consulting Psychology Press, 1967; rept., 1981).

6. Theodore Geisel (Dr. Seuss), "The Zode" (unpublished manuscript).

7. H. Stephen Glenn and Jane Nelson, *Raising Self-Reliant Children in a Self-Indulgent World* (Rocklin, Calif.: Prima Publishing, 1987), 40.

8. David Elkind, *All Grown Up and No Place to Go* (Reading, Mass.: Addison-Wesley, 1984).

9. Robert Laurent, *Keeping Your Teen in Touch with God* (Elgin, Ill.: David C. Cook, 1988), 12.

Barriers to Developing
Leadership Ability in Students

I F DEVELOPING STUDENT LEADERSHIP HAS so many benefits and is so easy, why aren't we doing it? Because, unlike much of what we do in youth ministry, there are some built-in obstacles that come with the territory. Developers of leadership in the average youth ministry will encounter several recognizable barriers.

The minute you begin a leadership program you will get flak. This opposition may come from several areas. My first experience in designing a leadership development program nearly cost me my life as a youth minister. Believing that the kids in our church needed a challenging experience, I designed a program that included frequent meetings and high responsibility and called for total commitment. I was so consumed with sharpening the program, setting the meeting dates, and planning the leadership retreat that I forgot to get feedback from the church staff and the parents.

When I passed out the program brochure, the positive responses from the students were overwhelming. The kids ate it up when I announced it. Most of them were ready for a challenge and were willing to sacrifice lots of homework and yard work time to fulfill the requirements.

The response of the parents was considerably less enthusiastic. I had allowed them no input and, as a result, their support was conspicuously absent. Because of my inability to rally parental backing, the parents of several key students wouldn't let their kids enter the program. And not only did I receive flak from parents, but the church board and pastoral staff were also unhappy about not being consulted. People in positions of leadership don't like surprises. Much of the flak I caught designing my first program was well deserved. Several of the meeting dates conflicted with church events. This could have been avoided if I had included the parents and the church staff in the planning process.

Another area where you will encounter flak will come from the students. When you begin to build student leadership teams, for the first time you will not be working with the whole group. Leadership teams

29

by their nature are small groups. Not every student is involved and it usually doesn't take long for cries of favoritism to surface. Some of the uninvolved students will voice it, but many will feel it. Feedback like that from students is usually enough to stop sensitive youth workers in their tracks. Flak and criticism hurt, whether they're from the staff, the parents, or the kids.

Let me suggest two good rules for dealing with flak. First, take the time to learn from it. You may be at fault. My student leadership development process was much more effective the second time around. The input from the staff and the parents, although painful, was very instructive in designing future programs.

Second, don't allow criticism and flak to paralyze you. The average American hears fourteen negative comments for every positive one. If you're anything like the average youth worker, you only remember the negative feedback anyway. Criticism comes with the territory of leadership. Evaluate it and use it, but don't let it paralyze you.

Most youth workers are so busy, we program our ministries by pressure instead of by priorities. Most paid and volunteer youth workers have one thing in common—too much to do and too little time in which to do it. The average youth worker's time generally breaks down into three major responsibilities.

> 1. *Responsibility for Program Development*
>   Sunday school
>   Camps and retreats
>   Weeknight meetings
>   Bible studies
>
> 2. *Responsibility for Problem Management*
>   Counseling
>   Solving problems with programs, people, parents, and the pastor
>
> 3. *Responsibility for People Development*
>   Mentoring
>   Selecting
>   Encouraging
>   Training future leaders

I discovered in my early years of youth ministry that I was so overwhelmed by the first two activities that there was little time left for intentional development of people. To be honest, I didn't have time to even think about it. Developing student leaders takes thought and time and is often squeezed out by other pressures. Identifying, motivating, training, and developing student leaders is a lot like prayer—essential for long-term spiritual health, but easy to skip when pressured.

Looking back, I realize that often I was the most formidable barrier to developing leaders. The first barrier that stops many of us is fear of failure. A youth ministry in the hands of capable adults usually runs pretty smoothly. Turn the same program over to a teenager and things may never go smoothly again. I learned this lesson the hard way. A group of student leaders at our small church in Duarte, California, decided to do a series of junior high outreach breakfasts. The first three ran pretty smoothly. The students did a great job of programming, the promotion was excellent, and the attendance grew from fifteen to over 100 students. For the fourth breakfast, their gala Christmas celebration, one of the students dressed up like Rudolph the Red-Nosed Reindeer. During the skit, Rudolph slipped and gored a kid in the forehead. Fifteen minutes later, I am at the hospital trying to explain to the doctor and the kid's parent how this kid was gored by Rudolph the Red-Nosed Reindeer at our church breakfast. Giving significant leadership responsibility to students often has the comfortable feel of a casual stroll through a mine field, and when they fail, we are the ones who hear about it.

Another obstacle is the Messiah complex that can come with a seminary degree. The lack of contemporary Christian lay leadership could be explained by a sign seen hanging in a church office: "Pastors are paid to be good, the rest of us are good for nothing." The average church often hires a youth pastor to rob the students of the opportunity to develop their gifts for ministry. The Messiah complex usually plays itself out with two results, both of which inhibit students from developing as leaders.

The first result is the tendency to control. Phrases like "If you want something done right, you've got to do it yourself" describe well the tendency to keep a firm lock on every facet of the ministry.

The second result is the tendency to rescue, which stops the developmental process that is so essential to producing leaders. Failure is seldom fatal and is often a strategic tool used by God for instruction and character development. The experience of failure brings opportunity for instruction and training and also communicates clearly the critical lesson that actions lead to consequences. Rescuing usually makes our youth ministries look better, but it retards the growth of our student leaders.

Another barrier is the love affair we have with the size of the youth ministry. Find any gathering of youth workers and the number one question asked is usually, "How many kids do you have in your youth group?" Many of us do not realize that if we have more than a handful of kids we may have more than we could ever develop. Jesus spent the better part of three years working full time with twelve people.

A nationally known Christian leader, after hearing me speak on this issue, pulled me aside and said, "I became a leader because my youth group was so small. We had four kids in our youth group and my freshman year our youth leader announced that we needed a youth group president. Because of my shyness, I sat in my chair praying that it wouldn't be me. He then announced that the new president was the student who sat in the chair with the 'X' marked on the bottom of it. I turned the chair over and nearly died when I found the 'X.' I started leading that year—it's been thirty years and I haven't stopped since." He then looked at me and said, "You know, I never would have had the opportunity to develop as a Christian leader if I had been in a large youth group."

Another barrier to developing leadership is the tendency we have to give more responsibility than students can handle. Many teenagers are already unbelievably busy. To contemporary kids, stress is not just a psychological term—it's a fact of life. School, sports, jobs, family, homework, friendships, and church programs are just some of the activities already on the frenzied schedules of today's teenagers. Unfortunately, when it comes to developing student leadership, many churches operate on this dual philosophy: "Recruit 'em if they're breathing—kill 'em if they're dedicated." Effective development will help students maintain a balanced life.

Furthermore, we often don't believe in the capability of teenagers. The bad news is that the minute we decide to begin developing leaders and start shopping for leadership candidates we often find that the shelves are empty. Most of our kids come closer to being "ain'ts" than saints. The good news is that Jesus had the same problem. Check out the motley crew that we call the disciples. You've got them all in your youth group. Look at Peter: always causing trouble, with both feet permanently planted in a rather oversized mouth. He's the kid in your youth group you are praying will at least shut up. Worse still, you've probably got a Thomas. He's the kid who throws cold water on every one of your great ideas with the phrase, "This is stupid and it will never work." He's the kid you are praying will move. Many of us are stopped because we can't see the potential in our students.

Some of us believe in teenagers, but we doubt our own abilities to develop leaders. We feel inadequate, doubt our own leadership skills, and are pretty convinced that if we did launch a leadership program the students would stay away in droves. This type of thinking comes from the false assumption that leaders produce leaders. Nothing could be further from the truth. Strong leaders often produce far more followers than leaders. The main ingredient necessary for developing a leadership team is encouragement, not personal giftedness. If you can love kids, you can build leaders! In Chapter Four, we will look at an encouraging example of how the model of love and compassion nurtured the leadership abilities of a student.

Creating an Environment for Leadership Development

A GROUP OF CHURCHES IN THE Pacific Northwest recently completed a church growth study of more than sixty churches. They studied statistics for attendance, age, and income, and then surveyed the attitudes and thought processes of the leaders. They discovered that "whether a church was static or growing depended directly on the attitudes of the leaders." Where the church leaders were positive, flexible, confident, cheerful, and goal-oriented, the churches were vibrant, alive, and growing. But where the leaders had little vision or creativity and few exciting goals, the churches were stagnant and paralyzed.[1]

In leadership development, as in life, growth takes place best when environmental conditions are conducive to growth. Most of the strategies in this book can be modified, but there are certain factors that are essential to creating a climate for leadership development.

Believe that kids are capable. I recently had a conversation with a high school principal in Denver, in charge of a student body of 2,000, who told me that he was led to Christ by a sophomore girl at his school. Evidently her youth worker believed that she was gifted, was worth training, and could have an effective ministry leading her friends to Christ. Teenagers are capable of having an incredible impact for Christ and that capability is often unlocked when an adult finds an area of strength and calls attention to it.

Believe that Christ's call to service includes teenagers. The call to the Christian life is the call to service. For years teenagers have been taught that they are "the church of tomorrow." Most teenagers aren't even sure there will be a tomorrow. This only serves to excuse teenagers from hearing the call of Christ in the present. Nowhere in Scripture does Jesus say, "Come, serve me. Tomorrow will be fine." Teenagers need to hear the call of Christ to service today. They need to believe that their service, gifts, and abilities are needed now. Let them serve on the church board. Invite their participation in the services. Expect them to give financially. Insist that they vote in the congregational meetings. Take them seriously and they will begin to take service in the church seriously.

Create a motivational environment through vision. Vision leads to enthusiasm and enthusiasm is a motivator. Vision is seeing people in terms of their potential. Vision was a critical key in the leadership development ministry of Jesus. Jesus saw a writer in a tax collector, a great preacher in a bigmouthed fisherman, and a man of faith in a doubting Thomas. In fact, Jesus tipped his hand when he called the disciples by declaring, "Come, follow me, and I will make you fishers of men" (Matthew 4:19). That's the key to vision and motivation. Jesus was more focused on what the disciples could become than what they were in the present. Show me a youth worker who is focused on what his or her kids are like now, and I will show you a discouraged youth worker. Conversely, the person who is focused on what his or her kids can become will discover a remarkable ability to stay encouraged. If you want to become a person who brings out the best in others, focus on their futures and look at them through the eyes of faith. In that kind of environment kids will be convinced they can become someone great for God.

Years ago, a friend told me the story of a group of people living in a small town at the bottom of a little valley in Maine. They were informed they had only a year left of life in the town. The government was building a dam at the end of the valley, and in a year the town would be several hundred feet underwater. The choice was clear, move or buy very good scuba equipment. Anyone visiting the town about nine months later would have been shocked at the transformation. People were still living there, but the once quaint, beautiful little hamlet had become a depressed ghost town. Why paint a house, mow a lawn, or fix a fence if it all was going to be destroyed? The lesson is painfully clear. *Where there is no faith in the future there is no power in the present.* Believing in kids may well be our greatest contribution to them, because often our vision and faith in the future of our students is the key that encourages and motivates them.

Believe in your own ability to develop students. Youth workers often shy away from developing students not because they question the capabilities of the students, but because they question their own capabilities. Somehow, even in the face of our own experiences, we think we need advanced degrees in human development to help a kid discover his of her gifts and potential for ministry. Early in my years in youth ministry, a wise older Christian pulled me aside and told me that kids coming into the youth group really only need two things—*a warm welcome and an adult who's crazy about them.* Your capacity to develop kids will only be limited to your ability to love them.

Create a motivating environment through affirmation. Most of us are trained to only remember the negative feedback we hear, not the positive. Leadership development is the art of catching the students doing something right. Be quick to encourage and slow to criticize. Most students attract attention only when they act out in unhealthy ways. Youth ministries ought to be centers of celebration. Stephen Glenn states that, "Any positive movement in the right direction, if it is received in the spirit of celebration, will produce more movement in that same direction."[2]

Have a specific vision for how kids' capabilities can be realized. Kids need specific responsibilities. That's why the ministry team assignments are so effective.

Recently, while speaking at a high school conference in Jackson, Mississippi, I met two remarkable high school students. These young ladies were two of the sharpest, most motivated high school juniors that I have met in a long time. They cornered me for lunch and wanted advice with their ministry. They told me that they were coleading a weekly on-campus Bible study for sixty junior high girls. They were planning a retreat and wanted advice on how to put one together. These two girls couldn't have been more motivated. They were loving junior high kids, leading a Bible study, and dreaming about putting together and running their first retreat—all at age sixteen. I later found out that during the previous year their youth pastor asked them to lead a small group of junior high girls in a Bible study. They started with six kids and the rest is history. Their lives and the lives of a lot of junior high girls changed the very minute a youth pastor got specific. Kids need significant, specific responsibilities. That is often the key that unlocks the door of opportunity to developing gifts for leadership.

Have patience. When you work with teenagers, you have to wonder if spending your standard sixty hours a week teaching, counseling, preparing, calling, and hanging out with kids will ever pay off. Few youth leaders realize such a reward without putting in a lot of years with one church. Art Erickson has invested twenty-three years in the young people of Park Avenue United Methodist Church in Minneapolis, where he is associate pastor and president of the Park Avenue Urban Program and Leadership Foundation. Art received a letter from a former youth group member of twenty years ago who grew up in an urban neighborhood two blocks from the church. This boy overcame seemingly insurmountable odds in an extremely dysfunctional family; married; earned a Ph.D. in counseling, and is now in private practice. I think this letter is maybe as much your letter as Art's.

The Counselor's Tent

Dear Art,

I've planned this letter for a number of years now, and the occasion of celebrating your twentieth year as youth minister of our church gives me the extra boost that I need to get it written. Actually, I've wanted to write a research paper about the youth program and you, and I hope that some day I can spend some quality time on a project like that. I guess this letter will focus more on you because, when I think back into my childhood and adolescence where most of my personality and spiritual growth took place, it was you who occupied a very important place during that period of my life. It's been a special treat to have gotten to know your wife these last few years, and she seems like icing on the cake to a relationship that has been with me so long in the person of yourself.

When I think about what you mean to me, it's hard to put into words—similar to what I'd say if asked what my mother or father means to me. For you are to me one of those symbolic persons each of us has—people who become almost larger than life to us emotionally because of how deeply they affect us during an intense period of our lives.

I met you when I was ten. I've known you for twenty years—two-thirds of my life. I went on canoe trips with you, slept in tents with you, climbed mountains with you, saw your anger, saw your pain, your laughter, your joy. I saw you get mad at kids who deserved your anger and then watched you laugh with them—and I wondered why you forgave them. I saw you live in an emotional crucible and wondered where you got the strength to continue reaching out when you were hurting so much inside. You became someone I idolized, someone I respected, someone I rebelled against—someone I eventually tried to understand in terms of what your life has stood for.

We psychologists use the term *introject* to describe one whom we have emotionally and symbolically "taken into" our own personality. An introject is an interior "person" who in many ways is always with us, who silently looks over our shoulder as we go through life, who criticizes or praises us, who loves us or scolds us. An introject becomes an inherent part of who we are emotionally and consequently affects us more deeply than any books, sermons, or speeches could ever affect us.

You are one of my introjects. You are an introject who has been faithful; you are an introject who has steadily cared; you are an introject who has become an interior measuring stick for the most important things in my life. Above all, you are an introject of Jesus Christ for me.

Here's what I remember when I think of you: you never slept in the counselor's tent. Remember where the grown-ups went to get away from the kids—where they went to recoup their sanity and emotional balance after a long day spent with us? Where they could shut us out and talk grown-up talk with each other, play cards, have a good time by themselves? I always felt a little lonely when the counselors were in their tent.

But you never slept there. I was often curious why you of all the grown-ups always ended up with us kids—why you, for some odd reason, decided you liked the noise, the mold, the smelly socks more than the camaraderie, adultness, and quiet cleanliness that resided in the counselors' tent. I had a hunch that, deep down inside, you might really enjoy getting away.

Yet for some odd reason, you didn't.

You were there in our tent when I was twelve, talking with us about girls, sex, and what real love was like, when other grown-ups thought we didn't care about that stuff at that age. You were there in our tent when I was thirteen, had just become a Christian, and was awkwardly putting on the new "clothes" of a relationship with Christ. You were there in our tent in Cincinnati when I was fifteen and struggled with painful and awkward feelings about whether I was lovable or not. You were there in our tent when I was eighteen and out on the Colorado desert in the middle of nowhere, when we were all too tired from a day of walking twenty miles to care much about anything. You were there when I was twenty and confused and fed up with my role as a good Christian, when I smashed the car window with a water balloon in an expression of my unrecognizable anguish inside. You stayed in my tent through all of that stuff.

I often wondered about that habit you had of sleeping in our tent, even though the stuff in there was pretty grimy. I know now why you chose to do that and what it meant. I have something emotionally and spiritually from your being in my tent that I will cherish the rest of my life.

Thanks for caring and being there in that place for me.

Leadership planning, programming, teaching, training, and delegating are all essential, but will never take the place of the ministry of being there for kids.

Endnotes

1. Gary Inrig, *Hearts of Iron, Feet of Clay* (Chicago: Moody Press, 1979), 55-56.

2. H. Stephen Glenn and Jane Nelson, *Raising Self-Reliant Children in a Self-Indulgent World* (Rocklin, Calif.: Prima Publishing, 1987), 87.

Strategy: A Youth Worker's Guide to Leadership Development

MOTIVATE: Getting Students Excited About Service and Leadership

EARLY IN MY YOUTH MINISTRY (light years ago), I had pretty well figured out that the way to develop character and commitment was to build a committed leadership core. I also thought that accomplishing that wasn't all that tough. I had spent five years as a volunteer in a large, growing youth ministry and had seen scores of high school students march bravely forward every time there was an opportunity to be in the expanding leadership core. It looked so easy. Two simple steps. Design a program, give a stirring call to commitment, and wham—students rise from every corner of the church just dying to join up and make an impact. Then I tried it on my own.

I was the youth pastor at a small church that numbered about 125 on a spectacular Sunday. The youth ministry had begun to grow, and the time had arrived to give these fortunate students the tremendous opportunity to be on my leadership team. With a vision of student leaders dancing in my head, I excitedly developed the program, ran off the applications, and announced the great opportunity. Our students were underwhelmed and stayed away in droves. I had a great time meeting by myself, which was a good thing because as I surveyed the wreckage of my defunct program, I discovered a fundamental leadership principle: *Motivation must precede selection.*

In the 1960s, a slogan often repeated was, "What if they had a war and nobody came?" A modification of that phrase may well describe the feelings of many youth workers as they wonder, "What if I started a ministry team and nobody showed up?"

Let's be honest. Students are not lining up to be selected for places of significant responsibility in the church or, for that matter, any other segment of society. For most of us looking to recruit and develop leaders, motivation is going to have to precede selection.

In the ensuing years, I've discovered and used five basic motivational principles designed to move students from apathy to involvement.

1. Students are motivated by personal exposure to the needs in the world. Many of our well-sheltered students are apathetic because most of their knowledge of the needs of the world comes from impersonal sources (TV, newspapers, movies, and so on). Like a new log thrown into an already burning fire, there is nothing like a personal encounter to ignite and motivate potential student leaders. Here are several ideas for getting students personally involved with the needs of the world.

HUNGER AND RELIEF EVENTS

One of the ways to bring the world into your church is to use good programs that deal with the themes of hunger and starvation. The following are two excellent organizations for these types of resources:

Compassion International, P.O. Box 7000, Colorado Springs, CO 80933. Compassion is a relief organization dedicated primarily to the care of children. Their program, "A Compassion Project," assists youth groups by promoting student involvement.

World Vision, 919 West Huntington Drive, Monrovia, CA 91016. A relief and development organization that has some great programs for building youth group awareness through fund-raisers, including the "Love Loaf" program and the "Planned Famine" program.

LIFE AUCTION

This game is designed to get students involved in thinking through their values. Divide your teenagers into small groups and give each group a copy of the list below. After each group finishes its sheet, bidding begins. When the auction is over, the whole group then discusses and evaluates what happened. The items below can be adapted to fit your particular group.

Life Auction

You have received $5,000 and can spend the money any way you desire. Budget the money in the column labeled "Amount Budgeted." We will then bid on each item, auction-style. Enter the highest amount you bid for each item in the "Amount Bid" column. You don't need to bid on every item. For those items you actually buy in our auction, enter the amount you pay in the "Amount Spent" column. It is your goal to gain the things you most desire.

LIFE DESIRES	AMOUNT BUDGETED	AMOUNT BID	AMOUNT SPENT
1. To have a wonderful family life without any hassles.	_____	_____	_____
2. To have all the money I need to be happy.	_____	_____	_____
3. To never be sick.	_____	_____	_____
4. To find the right mate, who is good-looking and fulfills me.	_____	_____	_____
5. To never have pimples.	_____	_____	_____
6. To be able to do whatever I want, whenever I want.	_____	_____	_____
7. To have all the power the president of a country has.	_____	_____	_____
8. To be the best looking person.	_____	_____	_____
9. To have a real hunger to always read the Bible.	_____	_____	_____
10. To be able to understand all things.	_____	_____	_____
11. To eliminate all hunger and disease in the world.	_____	_____	_____
12. To always be close to God.	_____	_____	_____
13. To never feel lonely or put-down.	_____	_____	_____
14. To always be happy and peaceful.	_____	_____	_____
15. To never feel hurt.	_____	_____	_____
16. To own a beautiful home, car, boat, plane, and seven motorcycles (one for each day of the week).	_____	_____	_____
17. To be super smart without ever having to attend school.	_____	_____	_____
18. To be able to excel and be superior in all things.	_____	_____	_____
19. To be filled with God's presence in the most dynamic way.	_____	_____	_____
20. To always know that I am in God's will.	_____	_____	_____
21. To be the greatest athlete in the world.	_____	_____	_____
22. To be admired by everyone else.	_____	_____	_____
23. To become a star on a popular TV show.	_____	_____	_____
24. To always have a lot of close friends who never let me down.	_____	_____	_____
25. To walk close to God.	_____	_____	_____

LOCKOUT

Instead of locking the kids in the church overnight, lock them out. Restrict them to a controlled area on the church grounds. Have boxes for them to sleep in, fire barrels or barbecues for them to stay warm around, and one (only one) chemical toilet on the grounds for their use. Do not provide running water.

Arrange for some people in your church to drive up and feed them a meal out of the back of the car. After their meal, let them experience a night out in the cold. You can plan a Bible study by flashlight related to God's concern for the poor.

Have your kids discuss the experience the next morning before they depart for home.

PRAYER TOUR OF THE INNER CITY

Load your kids into a church van and drive around the inner city. Pause in front of spots you've preselected and have your kids lead out in public prayer while they remain in the van. For example, you could stop in front of an abortion clinic; a skid row hotel; a group of prostitutes on a corner; a soup kitchen for the homeless; a rescue mission; a hospital; or a police station.

PRISON MINISTRY

Every city has jails, prisons, juvenile halls, reform schools, detention camps, and other such correctional institutions. One of the specific instructions Jesus gave the church was to minister to the needs of prisoners. It would not be an overstatement to say that to neglect this ministry would be an act of disobedience. Today most of our jails and prisons are filled to capacity with human beings who have been written off as "the least of these." The following ideas, suggested by Chuck Workman of Bravo Ministries in San Diego,[1] are just a few of the ways that your youth group—or your entire church—might become involved in a ministry to prisoners.

> • *Church Services.* The best way for a church or youth group to become involved is to provide a good church service within an institution. Because the U.S. Constitution guarantees each of us the freedom of worship, institutions are obligated to allow their residents this privilege. This doesn't grant a church the right to come in and use manipulation, intimidation, or the imposition of guilt, fear, and shame to bring the wicked to repentance. An

effective institutional church service should instead focus on the needs of the inmates without violating the rules of the institution and common decency. Special music, movies, and guest speakers can all be used, along with traditional singing and preaching, to bring a message of hope and salvation to the men and women. Far too often the church is considered irrelevant by both the staff and the inmates. Good planning and a sense of caring and responsibility can help counteract that perception.

• *Book Drives.* Many libraries in institutions are in terrible shape; the selection is poor and the condition of the books is worse. Churches frequently donate Bibles and religious reading material, but these often pile up in storerooms, ignored. A youth group could offer a tremendous service to an institution by providing books for its library. The institution may have a list of books it needs; if not, the youth group could put together its own list. Include classic books by the world's greatest authors; "how-to" books on languages, typing, and bookkeeping; and books on law, philosophy, ethics, history, and other subjects. A practical gift like this would make a profound impact on both the staff and the residents and would do much to improve the church's image.

• *Special Music.* The church has been faithful in providing good religious music, but inmates are often starved for music that is simply entertaining. Music is often an inmate's only communication with the outside world and may be his or her only means of emotional escape. A church or youth group could provide some regular entertainment that would not compromise the principles of the church.

• *Big Brother/Big Sister Programs.* It is often possible to pair up an inmate (especially younger ones) with a person from the community who would act as a "big brother" or "big sister." In fact, there may be a similar program already established in your area; if not, you can always create your own. Loneliness can be crippling in an institution, and the presence of a "friend" can make a world of difference in an inmate's adjustment. Once the prisoner is released, having concerned individuals and a strong church that offers some support is a real encouragement to stay clean and survive.

• *Pen Pals.* For those who can't or don't want to be involved with the inmates in person, letter writing can be a very good ministry. Inmates are avid writers; many write so often that obtaining enough postage becomes a problem. Receiving a letter during mail call can be the high point of the day. For churches that don't have a correctional institution close by, this is one way to reach behind the walls and touch someone's life. It's also great for young people who may not be allowed in prisons because they are underage.

• *Guest Speakers.* Institutions aren't usually intellectually stimulating, and churches could perform a real service by providing good speakers once in a while. There are some excellent speakers (not preachers) who would be very well received in a prison, such as public figures, politicians, sports figures, people from the entertainment industry, educators, former offenders, and attorneys.

• *Sports.* Most institutions have some type of intramural sports program, but since inmates tend to play each other over and over, it gets boring after a while. Churches are usually welcome to bring in a group to play an institutional team in basketball, softball, volleyball, horseshoes, chess, checkers, or almost any game. It's great fun and it makes the residents feel part of society again.

• *Special Services.* Churches are usually storehouses of talent and can offer that talent to an institution for the benefit of the inmates. Medical doctors, attorneys, psychologists, dentists, teachers, and social workers can volunteer their services. Tradesmen can offer their skills in carpentry, wiring, and plumbing. Church members can volunteer to cook and sew for those without these skills. Virtually any talent can be employed to help those in need.

• *Special Gifts.* Even when the economy is booming, most institutions don't have much money to work with. Churches could buy the items most needed by an institution: a sound system, chairs, curtains, or sports equipment, to name a few. If there is no particular item the church wants to purchase, it might consider a cash gift to be used at the institution's discretion.

• *Political Activities.* Correctional institutions are caught in a tough position today. Society wants its offenders locked away for longer periods of time, yet refuses to approve funds for the construction of more or better prisons. The result is that more and more people are forced into institutions where the quality of life (which never was good) is seriously deteriorating. The church can do much to become knowledgeable and active in the field of correctional reform. This one area, more than any other, could build the credibility of the church among the institutional population. Lobbies, letters, rallies, speeches, and books could be used to help persuade voters and legislators to alleviate incredibly bad living conditions in prisons and ease the suffering of many hurting people.

All of these ideas are worth checking into. *Some are more appropriate for youth groups than others.* If you need more information about what is possible in your area, contact your local government office or talk to officials who work within the institutions (like the prison chaplain, if there is one). They will try to help you decide upon a project that would be appropriate for your group.

SLEEP IN A BOX

Take a supply of cardboard boxes with you on your next summer camp or retreat. At some point during the event, have your kids spend one night sleeping in a box, with nothing but their clothes and perhaps an old blanket for warmth.

The next morning have your group discuss what it felt like to live, for one night, like the thousands of people living in boxes in America.

SPONSOR A CHILD

Many high school and junior high students are involved in world relief programs that sponsor children. Many agencies, like World Vision and Compassion International, try to find financial sponsors for children in orphanages overseas. These agencies will usually ask for a certain amount of money each month to provide food, clothing, and shelter for particular children. Most of the time, you can select a child to sponsor by name and receive detailed information about him or her, including photos and sometimes (after sponsoring) handwritten thank-you notes from the child.

If the sponsorship is too expensive for one student, why not ask your whole youth group to adopt one of these children and pledge to support the child monthly? Each person in the youth group can give a

49

certain amount (such as $1.00 per month). As the child's progress is monitored by the entire group, the group will really feel involved in that child's life. The group can also pray for the child on a regular basis. Not only is a project like this easy to do, it helps young people develop a world awareness and a sense of compassion for others.

VISIT AN INNER-CITY CHURCH

Take your kids to a Sunday service at an inner-city church. These churches range from small storefront congregations to large sanctuaries that hold thousands of people. Your kids will have the opportunity to rub shoulders with Christians from a different culture and experience a church service that may be quite unlike the one they're used to. On the ride home, discuss with your kids the similarities and differences between the congregations and services.

2. Students are motivated by involvement in service and missions. Service projects and mission trips motivate students! Not only are students exposed to the needs of the world, they also discover they have the potential to make an impact. Here are several ideas for getting your students involved in service and missions.

ADOPT A GRANDPARENT

This service project is great for young people who are mature enough to make a relatively long-term commitment. The first step is to take the entire group to visit a convalescent home or the homes of elderly people who are alone. Allow the kids to mingle and talk with these people so that they get to know them better.

Afterward, introduce them to the idea of "adopting" one or more of these seniors as a grandparent. Each young person would be assigned or would choose one or two elderly people to befriend, to visit on a regular basis, to remember on special occasions, and to take on short trips now and then. The adoption should continue for a specific amount of time, perhaps a year or longer.

During the course of the program, the young people could share with each other how things are going and what problems they are encountering. The youth sponsors would monitor the program and offer help and encouragement to the kids involved. At the end of the term, or at least once a year, the group could sponsor a special banquet or some other gathering where each young person brings his or her grandparent. Of course, some people may be unable to attend because they are confined to beds or nursing care, but others could attend. Most young people will find this to be a very rewarding experience, and the elderly people involved will greatly appreciate it.

BIG BROTHERS/BIG SISTERS

Your high school and college young people may want to become "big brothers" or "big sisters" to children in your church or neighborhood who don't have "real" older brothers and sisters. This could be as simple as getting to know them by name and making a point to welcome them each Sunday at church or to pay special attention to them in some way. It might include visiting them at home regularly, planning special activities, or picking them up for Sunday school. The teens could teach the children a skill—drawing, playing the guitar, fishing, carpentry, or cooking. It's a wonderful way for your teenagers to be positive role models for younger kids.

CALENDAR PAYOFF

Print a calendar that has a space for each day of the month. In each space, enter an instruction that will determine how much money each teen must give that day. The instruction should be humorous and should vary in amount from one day to the next. Allow a space on the calendar where kids can write how much they owe each day. They can then total it up at the end of the month. You might add one extra space allowing them to give any amount they choose. This approach adds a little fun and variety to giving.

When the month is up, the kids bring in the money they owe. Give the money to a local mission project.

A variation of this would be to print the instruction for each day on separate sheets of paper, fold them, and staple them so they are concealed until the end of the day. The instruction can then be a "fine" for certain things done or not done. For example, it might say, "Pay 5 cents for each class that you were late to today," or "Pay 25 cents if you forgot to brush your teeth."

Calendar Payoff

1. One cent for each pair of shoes and sneakers you own.
2. Three cents if you disobeyed your parents today.
3. Five cents if you forgot to use a deodorant today.
4. Four cents if you have blue eyes.
5. Ten cents if you did not clean your room today.

6. Fifteen cents if you did not attend church today.

7. Five cents if you washed your hair today.

8. One cent for each time you talked on the telephone today.

9. Five cents if you got up before seven a.m. today.

10. Three cents if you wore any type of jeans today.

11. Once cent for each soda you drank today.

12. Two cents for each hour of sleep you had last night.

13. One cent for each mile you live away from your church.

14. Two cents if you have a hole in your socks.

15. Five cents if you did not do your homework today.

16. Fifteen cents if you wore the color red today.

17. Two cents if you have your driver's license.

18. Four cents if you have brown eyes.

19. One cent for each letter in your last name.

20. Ten cents if you shaved anything today.

21. Five cents if you wore blue today.

22. Five cents for each test you had today.

23. One cent for each class you had today.

24. Fifty cents if you were not at teen choir tonight.

25. Ten cents if you did not eat breakfast at home this morning.

26. Three cents for each time you failed to make your bed this week.

27. Twenty cents if you did not donate any money yesterday.

28. Ten cents if you have a pair of Nike sneakers.

29. Three cents for each pair of gloves you own.

30. Three cents if you didn't read your Bible today.

31. Ten cents because it is almost the last day to pay.

CELL MINISTRY

Many youth workers struggle to create a New Testament fellowship within the social-cultural context of the established church program. The following is a solution. Meet once a week with a "cell group"—a handful of mature kids who are serious about growing and caring for others in the body of Christ. Spend the first hour in careful Bible study and the second hour in fellowship, sharing hurts and victories, and praying for one another. Each of these kids in turn builds a cell of kids that can meet together during the week. They can use the same material used in the original cell group. Thus, a network of behind-the-scenes fellowship and discipleship meetings takes place to supplement the normal program.

FREE CHILD CARE

A youth group in Massachusetts sponsors a once-a-month ministry to the parents in the community. They have named the program, "Get Out of Jail Free." On the first Saturday night of the month, the kids provide babysitting and child care services. Some of the students staff the church nursery and the rest put on a Vacation Bible School for the older kids. The service to the adults of the church is free, and the whole evening is planned, staffed, and run by the youth group. This is a great way for students to discover a variety of their own gifts and abilities in the context of service.

H.O.P. CLUB

H.O.P. stands for "Help Older People," and the H.O.P. Club is a program where teens and adults work together to assist the elderly with work that they are unable to do for themselves. Skilled adults train the youths to do carpentry, plumbing, wiring, upholstery, or whatever needs to be done, and they give direction and supervision while on the job. Younger kids can be involved in such tasks as washing windows and walls, raking leaves, shoveling snow, moving furniture, and writing letters. Many other people who want to be less directly involved can provide financial and other forms of assistance. The important thing is that the program be well-organized and regularly carried out. Many senior citizen groups can provide information on where the greatest needs are, and the elderly community can be informed that this service is available at little or no charge to them.

A program such as this not only provides valuable relief for the elderly, who normally must pay to have this work done, but it also offers kids the opportunity to give of themselves in a meaningful way and to build relationships with a segment of society that they often ignore.

SATURDAY SERVANTS

To give your youth group a regular chance to serve church members with special needs, designate occasional Saturday mornings (9:00 a.m. to noon) as the time for "Saturday Servants." Use a bulletin insert announcing the project two weeks beforehand so church members who need assistance can call the church ahead of time with their requests.

"Saturday Servants" focus primarily (although not necessarily exclusively) on performing chores for the elderly, shut-ins, widows, divorced people, and single parents in the church. Jobs might be anything from yard work to child care, car maintenance to furniture moving. It's a good idea to ask the people being served to provide the necessary equipment and cleaning supplies (if possible).

Your youths will find that their sacrifice of time and energy on a Saturday morning can provide a significant and practical ministry to many members of the church.

SERVANT CERTIFICATE

The servant certificate is a great way to get students involved in service projects in a fun, nonthreatening way. A sample certificate follows.

Servant Certificate

The bearer of this certificate is hereby entitled to one unabashed, unheralded gift of service to be lovingly performed by me at your point of need and time of convenience. Just let me know!

To:_____

From: _____, your humble servant,

this _____ day of _____ 19_____.

Mark 10:42-45

SERVANT SEARCH

Here's a service project that will challenge your kids to creative servanthood. Divide your large group into small groups of two or three. Tell the teenagers they have exactly one hour to circulate around the community and serve it in some fashion. The goal is to serve as many people as possible in any way possible. Be creative: Some students will sweep the sidewalks, others will go door-to-door asking to wash windows or pull weeds, and others will pick up trash in a local parking lot or field. Some may even go to a local gas station and pump gas for people at the self-serve island. No one is allowed to receive money for the services.

At the end of the hour, the students return to tell about their experiences. Award prizes for the most creative, hardest workers, most people served, and so on. Give lots of affirmation to each team. It will help build self-esteem in your students and encourage them to be self-starters.

STUDENT LED AND PLANNED MISSION TRIP

For overcoming apathy and enabling students to gain a vision of the potential for impact they possess, there may be no greater vehicle than a mission experience. Three essentials for maximum student impact are as follows:

1. Place the majority of the decision-making responsibility for the experience in the hands of the students.

2. Place the majority of the program or work responsibility in the hands of the students.

3. Bring the experience home with you. Students who plan meetings and handle great responsibility while on a mission trip can do the same in their own youth group.

An outstanding resource for students and youth workers is *The Complete Student Missions Handbook* by Ridge Burns with Noel Becchetti (Grand Rapids: YS/Zondervan, 1990).

3. Students are motivated by discovering their own gifts and potential. A lot of contemporary adolescents feel highly equipped to be perfectly useless. Often the focus in youth ministry is on the leader, not the kids. Student spectators in the average youth ministry watch as we conduct songs, make announcements, give stirring talks, and lead the whole meeting. As a result, kids leave our youth meetings impressed with our talents instead of having the opportunity to discover theirs. A key to motivating students is to enable discovery of their own gifts and abilities. A practical study on spiritual gifts may be just the key to helping some of our students begin to discover that they are both uniquely gifted and definitely needed.

The following resources are for a group exploration of the subject of spiritual gifts. These resources are designed to be highly experiential and discovery oriented.

Up Close and Personal by Wayne Rice (Grand Rapids: YS/Zondervan, 1990). This thirteen-week community building curriculum contains an excellent section on spiritual gifts, complete with worksheets and a leader's guide for each.

A Spiritual Gifts Test, from the Fuller Theological Seminary. Testing a wide variety of gifts found in the New Testament, this is a tool that will help the students examine their potential for ministry and leadership. Although the test is designed for adults, it has been used successfully with high school students. This test is best taken as a group, and it will require some interpretation and group application. To order the tests, call the Charles E. Fuller Institute of Evangelism and Church Growth at 1-800-999-9578.

STRENGTH VOTING

Another idea for building students' knowledge of their gifts and abilities is Strength Voting. This affirmation exercise helps them see their strengths through the eyes of others.

At the tops of their papers, ask the students to write their names and three things about themselves that they consider strengths. Warn them against excessive modesty; if they think they're good at something, tell them to be honest and write it down (examples: good listener, sense of humor).

When your kids are finished listing their virtues, ask them to pass the sheets around the room so that others in the group can "vote" on the strengths listed for each person. As a teen's sheet makes the rounds through the room, other group members mark a check by those qualities that they agree are prominent strengths. If a friend thinks a person has a strength that was not listed on the sheet but should be in the top three, then that friend should write in the strength. Lots of checks and probably lots of write-in votes will be added as the sheets circulate throughout the room. When the papers are returned to their owners, your kids will have a fairly clear idea of which strengths others see in them. Follow this up with a study on spiritual gifts and the call to service.

4. Students are motivated by exposure to people who believe in them. Today's students usually feel that adults are never on their side. The result is often a crisis of confidence that leads to apathetic indifference. Many of our students are not motivated because the overwhelming message heard from peers, adults, and the media is that they have nothing to contribute. Adolescents are starving for positive relationships with people who believe in them, their potential, and their futures.

The following ideas are geared to enable the development of close relationships between the youth worker and the students.

SECRET SPIRITUAL SPONSORS

To give your students a confidence-building experience with adults in your church, create a "Secret Spiritual Sponsor" (or "Adopt an Adolescent") program in which adults in the church are asked to sponsor (or adopt) a teenager in the youth group. The adults commit to support the young people with prayers, birthday cards, notes of encouragement and any other appropriate, meaningful ideas. Give sponsoring adults information cards on their youths; the cards are reminders as well as sources of information. At the end of the school year, organize a secret sponsor appreciation banquet as a thank-you to the adults. Introduce the teenagers to their sponsors and have them sit together at the banquet. A great follow-up idea is to have the teenagers sponsor younger kids at the church for the next year.

Sample Information Card

Name: Thomas Bishop

Address: 317 Canyon Road

City: Duarte, California

Phone: 555-0000

Birthdate: 9/16/73

Friends: Mark and Scott Johnston, Burt Burgess

Hobbies: Waterskiing, girls, basketball, *Sports Illustrated*

Comments: Thomas is a junior at North High School. He likes school enough to want to go to college, but is unsure as to where. Parents are Lynn and Tom, members of our church; brother is Tim, sister is Tammy. They moved here five years ago from Milwaukee.

STUDENT INVOLVEMENT PLANNING RETREAT

Students are amazed when an adult asks their opinions, much less includes them in a planning retreat. A great way to build relationships and confidence is to select a group of students and include them in the planning retreat for your ministry. Their confidence levels will rise and so will their ownership of the program. This can be done on a weekend retreat or a one-day brainstorming session.

TAKE STUDENTS TO MINISTRY TRAINING EVENTS

A great way to communicate to your students that they have leadership potential and to expose them to motivating speakers and ideas is to take a select group to an event designed to motivate and train youth workers. Events like the National Youth Workers Convention, National Resource Seminar, or other training conferences provide an atmosphere where the kids will be challenged to use their lives and make an impact. These types of events should be followed up by a debriefing, which will give you an opportunity to apply the material and evaluate the experience.

YOUTH LEADER'S COUPON BOOK

Most youth workers can't afford to give every young person in their group a Christmas or birthday present. Here's a gift idea that is economical as well as valuable. Create a coupon book that offers a variety of services to the young people and is redeemable any time during the year. Think up as many coupons as you like, such as the following:

- Good for one free dinner at my house.
- Good for one free rap session. Void between 11:00 p.m. and 7:00 a.m.
- Good for prayer for any prayer request.
- Good for one free ride (in an emergency) to the destination of your choice (within reason).
- Good for one encouraging word. Redeemable any time.
- Good for one free pat on the back when needed.
- Good for one pretty good answer to your most burning question.

Not only do these coupons offer the kids something for free, they also make the kids aware of the kinds of things you're willing to do for them.

5. Students are motivated as they are given responsibility. For many teenagers, youth ministry is a spectator sport. They watch as adults (many of whom are too busy anyway) frantically run around designing programs, planning meetings, leading songs and skits, and handling all of the major responsibilities for the youth group. In almost comical proportion, the harder the adults work, the more indifferent the students become. We often fail to realize that people are motivated by involvement. The giving of responsibility creates a sense of ownership, which often transforms the students' apathetic indifference to motivated involvement. Here are several ideas for involving students in leadership roles.

CHRISTIAN RESPONSIBILITY

The following is a list of responsibilities that Christians have to each other, according to the Bible. Pass the list out to your group, read the passages, and then try to answer the questions at the end.

Our Responsibilities to Each Other as Christians

Love One Another
Ephesians 5:1, 2
Romans 12:10
1 Peter 4:8
John 13:34, 35
John 15:12, 13
Hebrews 13:1
1 John 3:16, 17

Carry Each Other's Burdens
Romans 15:1
Galatians 6:2

Take Care of Each Other's Material Needs
Deuteronomy 15:7, 8
Romans 12:13

Confess Sins to One Another
James 5:16

Serve One Another
Galatians 5:13
Ephesians 5:21
1 Peter 4:9, 10

Pray for Each Other
Philippians 1:3-6
Ephesians 6:18
James 5:16

Be Patient with One Another
Ephesians 4:2

Discipline Each Other
Galatians 6:1, 2
Matthew 18:15
2 Thessalonians 3:14, 15

Worship Together
Psalm 95:6

1. How many of these responsibilities are being met in your group?

2. Is there one that surprises you or with which you disagree?

3. Is there one you are having difficulty doing?

4. Are these responsibilities optional or are they expected of all Christians?

5. Is there one you would like to work on as a group?

The meeting can be concluded by making a covenant with the other members of the group to work toward fulfilling one or more of the responsibilities. Close with a worship service or prayer of dedication for your new goals. It is helpful to set an evaluation date to check on your growth.

INCLUSIVE ELECTIONS

Youth group officers are the ones in many groups who run the meetings and plan the events. Often, however, officers are merely a group of close friends or the most popular teenagers. To prevent this and to give everyone an equal opportunity to serve, try some of these ideas.

1. List all the kids' names on separate slips of paper (mixed in with a sufficient number of blank slips, of course) and choose officers by allowing group members to draw the slips from a paper bag.

2. Let members write secretly who they think would be best for each office. (Youth leaders can sort out and appoint the choices.)

3. Before a meeting, write on note cards the offices to be filled, one officer per card. Tape the cards at random on the bottoms of several chairs in the youth room. When the kids enter the room and take their seats to begin the meeting, let them discover who the next slate of officers is.

4. Change officers every three months or so, and allow no one to hold an office more than once.

5. Only after everyone has served as an officer, hold a genuine election. By this time, group members have observed how different classmates perform and their votes will be wise ones.

JOBS FOR EVERYONE

To make those long, boring bus trips to a camp or special activity a fun experience for everyone, try this idea. Especially good for junior high kids, this is a good way to teach responsibility. Make up a list of "job opportunities" for every person on the bus. Mail the list to all the kids before the trip and give them the chance to apply for the positions on a first-come, first-serve basis. The following is a sample list of job descriptions:

Secretary. Keeps track of pertinent information supplied by the odometer orator, the timekeeper, the driver, the personal secretary, and others, in order to write "The Story of Our Work Camp Experience." Will keep and collate all information from the others at the end of the trip.

Bus Attendant #1. Checks oil and adds if necessary, inspects for underhood leaks or malfunctions, assists in gassing the bus, checks front lights and safety signals.

Bus Attendant #2. Checks tires, rear lights, and safety signals; assists in gassing the bus; records gallons/liters and cost.

Personal Secretary. Keeps track of humorous and interesting stories of our activities to, from, and during our trip.

Environmental Control Technician #1. Ensures that the center aisle and the right side of the bus (facing the front) are kept free of debris. Checks that all windows on the right side of the bus are closed at the end of the trip. Periodically passes a wastebasket to messy passengers.

Environmental Control Technician #2. Ensures that the center aisle and the left side of the bus are kept free of debris. Checks that all windows on the left side of the bus are closed at the end of the trip. Keeps track of the messiest person, who must help clean the bus when we get home.

Security Engineer #1. Makes sure the bus is not tampered with at rest stops. Stands guard while Security Engineer #2 is pursuing necessary comforts.

Security Engineer #2. Makes sure the bus is not tampered with while Security Engineer #1 pursues necessary comforts.

Sound Technician #1. Supervises the operation of the radio or tape deck: volume, balance, tone, rewind.

Sound Technician #2. Supervises the selection of tapes, relying on passenger input and sensitivity. Checks tapes and sees that they are placed in proper cases. Assists Sound Technician #1 with any complex operational procedures.

Timekeeper. Keeps track of time from departure to arrival. Clocks the amount of time spent at rest areas, food establishments, and so on.

Assistant Timekeeper. Assists timekeeper by arranging chronological particulars, and helps timekeeper with simultaneous timings of who spends the most time in the bathrooms, who sleeps the most, and other important observations.

Official Nose Counter. Counts noses to make sure no one has more than one, and reports directly to the driver when all noses are accounted for. We do not discriminate against people without noses, but we ask that you please wear one (plastic acceptable) in order to be counted.

Odometer Orator. Records odometer readings of miles traveled, and reports them to the timekeeper for recording. Lets us know how many miles between rest stops, food stops, gas stops, and the mileage for the entire trip, start to finish.

Assistant to the Driver. Assists driver with map reading, conversation, and conveying messages to passengers. Receives a portion of all snacks to feed the driver. (It is very unfair to smell chocolate and not receive any!) Also enforces the "no taco chips or corn chips" rule. (Taco chips and corn chips stink on a hot bus!)

Recreation Director. Keeps our ride from getting boring by involving us periodically in recreational activities such as games, songs, quizzes, and skits.

Interior Recreation Assistant #1. Assists Recreation Director in leading games and coordinating resources for activities. Reports on nonparticipants of group games for public embarrassment later. Right side of the bus only.

Interior Recreation Assistant #2. Assists Recreation Director in leading games and coordinating resources for activities. Reports on nonparticipants of group games for public embarrassment later. Left side of the bus only.

All travelers shall be employed as Stupidity Discouragers. Read here what is stupid!

1. It is stupid to litter inside or outside the bus.

2. It is stupid to be so loud on the bus that everyone gets a headache.

3. It is stupid to stick anything out the bus window (arms, legs, heads, hands, friends).

4. It is stupid to bring soft drinks on the bus (ice water is okay).

5. It is stupid to buy Big Gulps, Slurpies, or gallon-size drinks because no one's bladder is large enough to contain them.

6. It is stupid to do anything unsafe.

You'll find that kids will take pride in their jobs and do them with enthusiasm. At gas stops, for example, the kids will act as a regular pit crew, jumping out of the bus, taking care of all its vital functions, and recording information. If you need to accommodate more people, you can come up with a few more creative jobs: chief tire thumper, on-board photographer, visual perception technician (cleans windshield at rest stops), or whatever.

SUMMER EXCHANGE PROGRAM

This idea is patterned after foreign exchange programs that are common in public high schools and is designed to give students real responsibility in a ministry setting. The same thing can be done between churches in neighboring towns, states, or even other countries. An exchange program trades individual young people between two churches for a short period of time (one month is ideal). The exchange need not be simultaneous (yours may go in June; theirs may come in July). The young person who is traded then becomes an apprentice to the youth minister at the new church. While he or she is there, that young person will learn to develop leadership skills and to share his or her abilities with another part of the body of Christ.

Your church and the exchanging church must be clear on the duties of the youths. These may include working in the office, running errands, planning youth nights, working on files, helping with visitation, leading Bible studies, giving devotionals, helping with Vacation Bible School, or just being a part of the regular youth program. Try to immerse the youth in the program of the church without drowning him or her! If this is a full-time exchange, with the kids staying in the homes of church members, be sure that they have or can find their own transportation and that their schedules do not upset their "host families." The churches should provide some spending money and plan to pick up all church-related expenses, such as retreat costs and all youth activities.

To select a youth for this program, have anyone who is interested apply and write an essay, or give a brief biographical sketch with a Christian testimony. Send these to the exchange church and let it choose which applicant it would like to sponsor.

When your exchange student arrives, you might want to introduce him or her in your church service and present the youth with a key to the church, an honorary membership certificate, or some other token of welcome. This will give the youth maximum exposure to the congregation and may open avenues for service. Having a responsible and committed young person participate in your group may do wonders for your kids, and the leader that you send off will return with new perspectives and greater maturity in Christ.

YOUTH GROUP SCOUTS

Pair off selected members of your group and send them out to investigate other church youth groups. Tell the students to look for great ideas to bring back and implement in their own youth ministry. They can drive together to the meeting but, once on site, they must not talk to each other or sit together. This will give them an understanding of how visitors feel at their own youth group. You may want to arrange an interview meeting with the two investigators after they visit the other group.

YOUTH LED FAMILY NIGHT

This event uses youth leadership and talent for a family get-together at the church to emphasize family life in the home and in the family of Christ. Following the instructions in Exodus 37:1-9 (*The Living Bible* gives modern measurements), the group members are assigned (or assign themselves) the various tasks required to construct an actual size replica of the ark of the covenant, using plywood, jigsawed cherubim, and ring-type drawer pulls for handles. Every piece used is painted gold.

At the family night event, the kids improvise an informal drama (this is better than written and memorized) to depict a family altar or family worship time. Families enjoy seeing their kids act out what a Christian home can be like. For balance, Act One could include an exasperating marital experience that could actually stretch the unity of the marriage and home, letting Act Two be the family experience of worship where healing begins. Capsule cures for family problems should be avoided. Preferably one of the kids (or possibly the pastor) explains the significance of the ark on display. Apply it to the practical way in which God's presence is to be understood in a Christian home and church today.

YOUTH LED SENIOR HIGH CORPS GROUPS

A corps group is made up of twelve senior high youths interested in spending eight weeks working and praying together in intensive study. For every twelve youths who enlist, a new corps group is formed. These groups are designed for senior high youths who want more than the Sunday school class and the weekly youth meeting—youths who want to "dig" and discover the meaning of discipleship and put it into practice. The corps groups have a three-fold purpose of spiritual maturation; spiritual reproduction; and discipleship.

Within the corps groups of twelve, there is a breakdown of three groups of four with a student leader sitting in with each small group. Within the small groups, the following three commitments are made by each participating individual: a personal commitment to Jesus Christ; a personal commitment to fellow corps members; and a personal commitment to other Christians (the church) to work together to reach the world for Christ.

On the first evening, each young person shares the story of how he or she made a commitment to Christ with the other four individuals and then makes a commitment to the group members to pray for them daily, to be available if needed, and to put forth a special effort to get to know each person well during the eight-week period. It can be a moving experience. Each member of the corps group is expected to be at each meeting for the eight weeks. All absences must be excused prior to the meeting. During the meeting, there is a one hour discussion of the previous week's assignment. The second hour is spent in small groups discussing questions given out by the corps group leader.

Student leaders working with the corps groups are required to meet for one hour each week to go over the materials for that week. These students are briefed by the youth worker. Materials used include an assigned portion of Scripture to be studied during the week and any other books or materials that might be relevant. A typical weekly reading assignment might include the reading of an entire book of the New Testament (such as Galatians, Ephesians, or Timothy) or just the reading and re-reading of a Scripture passage. Ask the youths to turn in a paraphrased version of the portion of the Scripture they read. In addition to this, the kids would be asked to read a chapter or two from a book on spiritual growth, selected by the leader.

Endnotes

1. Chuck Workman, Bravo Ministries, 4817 Palm, La Mesa, CA 91942.

PLAN: Designing the Leadership Program

IMPLEMENTING A PROGRAM DESIGNED TO develop leaders can be a little dangerous because in most cases programs don't produce leaders—people do. Occasionally when we borrow a program that has worked effectively in another ministry setting, we discover that it doesn't work in ours. Without a plan, however, the best leadership developer in the world is bound to be ineffective. The key is to create a process that challenges *your* students, meets *their* needs for growth, and allows for maximum responsibility and accountability.

Many youth workers have found the following five steps essential to planning a leadership team:

1. Determine the goals, requirements, and dates for the leadership team.

2. Write job descriptions with specific expectations for the leadership team.

3. Schedule consistent meeting times.

4. Develop the content for the leadership retreat and team meetings.

5. Develop your student application packet.

I have included in this chapter all of the planning, promotional, and application forms we used in our leadership development ministry. Each situation is unique. What works well at the Crystal Cathedral may not work at my church because of the size difference. I first used these forms in a church of 125 and more recently at Marin Covenant Church, a church of 550. In both situations, these same five steps were helpful in designing the leadership process and they can be adjusted and adapted to meet most situations.

1. Determine the goals, requirements, and dates for the leadership team. Programs and ministries that are not guided by goals and objectives seldom make much of an impact. "Aim at nothing and you'll hit it every time" seems to describe much of the frenzied activity that takes place in contemporary ministry. The hard work of setting goals and objectives will give vision and direction to the leadership team. Students will know what they have joined and why they should pay the price of commitment.

Stating the vision positively in terms of commitment and potential for growth captures the imagination and lights a fire under prospective students. The average church kid is bored, underchallenged, and often just looking for the opportunity to be part of something that is going in exciting directions.

Our youth ministry at Marin Covenant set the following goals one year:

We believe that high school Christians should be

- *Informed*—therefore, we will spend time doing in-depth Bible study.

- *Articulate*—therefore, we will work at how to present Jesus Christ attractively and convincingly.

- *Compassionate*—therefore, we will be involved in programs that meet needs (Mexicali, Rest Home Ministry, Project Serve).

- *Supportive*—therefore, we will work at building good friend-ships.

The goals you have set will lead to the commitment level and requirements for the leadership team. Spell out the requirements clearly and be specific. Let these kids know exactly what they are joining. As you think through the requirements, don't be afraid to ask for commit-ment.

Many Christian kids are mired down in apathy because we have failed to make demands. Douglas Hyde suggests in *Dedication and Leadership* (see Appendix D) that the reason communism has been so successful in developing leaders is because it dares to make demands of its followers. Bold goals and high requirements that call for commit-ment often draw students looking for a challenge.

For my most recent youth ministry team, the requirements for join-ing the team were as follows:

S.A.L.T.—Student Action Leadership Team Requirements

1. You must be willing to work hard.

2. You must be a Christian who desires to follow Jesus Christ.

3. You must be committed to be at the S.A.L.T. meeting on time and bring a Bible, a notebook, and a pen.

4. You must be willing to support the high school events through your presence, prayers, and hard work.

5. The length of this commitment is from January 27 to June 3.

6. You will have responsibility for serving on one ministry team.

7. P.S. It would help if you like to have fun!

Once goals and requirements are set, the next step is to determine the starting and ending dates. Setting a specific length of commitment will give two advantages. First, students may be more willing to risk joining if they know the commitment has an ending date. Because contemporary teenagers are busy, they will be much more likely to make a commitment to a team that has a definite time period. Second, students may decide to wait for the next application time, and this will allow the youth worker to do preparation work designed to get them ready.

The length of commitment set by youth workers varies. Although some youth workers have traveled the year-long commitment route, I have found it helpful to recruit students for semesters. We usually recruited three leadership teams per year.

Ministry Team 1—Commitment dates: September 15-December 15

Ministry Team 2—Commitment dates: January 15-May 15

Summer Ministry Team—Commitment dates: June 15-August 15

Many of our students reapplied and were on the team for the whole year, but regular recruitment enabled us to add new students and change responsibilities—and it gave the kids (and me) a break in the process.

2. Write job descriptions with specific expectations for the leadership team. Leadership development will not happen without specific significant responsibility. Creating a variety of ministry positions will give

69

the students specific places to use their gifts and abilities. It is usually a good idea to list more jobs than you will actually have. This gives the students a broader choice of areas to serve. After the students have signed up, you can eliminate the ministry positions that weren't chosen. The sample list that appears later in this chapter may be helpful as you design your own ministry teams. We used it and then dropped the teams that generated the least interest.

3. Set consistent meeting times. Leadership team meetings will be most effective if they occur at a time when students are available and if they are held at a consistent time. Many have found it helpful to have leadership meetings twice per month. If possible, drop an ineffective program and use the time for your leadership program. In my last youth ministry, we canceled our Sunday evening program (which was really just a poor repeat of our Wednesday night) and replaced that with a weekly leadership meeting. This enabled us to meet with our student leaders on a weekly basis without adding another meeting to their already busy schedules.

4. Develop the content for the leadership retreat and team meetings. It was no accident that Jesus and his disciples spent so much time away. Leaders and leadership teams take time to develop and one of the best ways to build community and commitment is to start with a leadership development retreat. There are several significant benefits. The retreat will give you time to develop unity and give ownership to the students as you evaluate and plan the youth ministry and spend large amounts of time getting students involved in training and development. I discovered that I was able to spend more time with students in a single retreat than in three months of meetings. For more in-depth information on developing and leading a ministry training retreat, see the ideas in Appendix B.

One of the most positive developments in recent years is taking place in the field of youth ministry resources. There are now an overwhelming number of books, workbooks, tapes, videos, and conferences available to motivate and enable spiritual growth and leadership development. The key to effective content in team meetings is to use the material that matches up with your students' needs. I ask two questions when deciding what content to use. First, what are the needs of these students spiritually, relationally, personally, and developmentally? Second, which resources or combination of resources will best meet these needs?

Appendix C, "Content Ideas for Training Meetings," contains resources that have been used effectively in enabling spiritual growth and leadership development. This list is by no means complete, but it will serve as a guide when you look at resource options.

Although the design of the leadership team and its responsibilities may vary, it should maintain one constant—a high degree of commitment. Through the years, I have observed many of the students in my youth group exhibit a high degree of commitment to sports, academics, drama, choir, student offices, and class projects. Most of the time, that commitment built positive qualities of discipline and excellence into the students. Unfortunately, all too often that same quality of commitment doesn't translate into involvement in the church. Some of us operate off the philosophy that although the world may demand excellence, "anything is good enough for God." A generation of teenagers has the attitude that the church and Christian ministry need not be taken seriously. Calling students to commitment communicates that the Christian life and commitment to ministry are worth taking seriously.

The following worksheet should enable you to "put it all together" as you plan the leadership team.

Student Action Leadership Team
Program Planning Sheet

Names of Students likely to be involved in the team:

PROGRAM PLANNING

Goals. What are my main goals for the leadership team?

Requirements. What are the requirements for involvement in the team?

Leadership Positions. Write out the leadership positions and the job descriptions for each.

Schedule. Fill in the following:

Length of commitment:_____

to _____

Date of informational meeting:_____

Dates of the leadership retreat:_____

Team meetings will be ☐ Weekly ☐ Biweekly

Meeting times will be from _____ to _____

Our first meeting will be _____

Our last meeting will be _____

5. Develop your student application packet. How a student enters the leadership program will set the tone for the quality of the experience. A good application process will convince potential student leaders that this program is important and is to be taken seriously.

Sample forms from the promotional application packet that we used to recruit and select student leaders are shown on the following pages.

- Cover sheet with goals and requirements
- Servant leader application
- Reference sheet
- Ministry team job descriptions
- Leadership involvement application survey
- Leadership retreat registration form

Student Action Leadership Team
High School Leadership Teams

IN THE HIGH SCHOOL DEPARTMENT we are committed to developing the leadership skills of our students. Because of this, we are forming several key Student Leadership Teams, composed of high school students who are interested in serving the Lord in the high school ministry.

For this experience to be a positive one, anyone seeking to be on a leadership team will need to consider the following requirements, then fill out the application and reference forms attached and return them no later than _____ .

There will be an informational meeting on

_____ for interested students and parents.

S.A.L.T. Goals

We believe that high school Christians should be

- *Informed*—therefore, we will spend time doing in-depth Bible study.

- *Articulate*—therefore, we will work at how to present Jesus Christ attractively and convincingly.

- *Compassionate*—therefore, we will be involved in programs that meet needs (Mexicali, Rest Home Ministry, Project Serve).

- *Supportive*—therefore, we will work at building good friendships.

S.A.L.T. Requirements

1. Must be a student who takes living the Christian faith seriously

2. Must attend most high school events
   a. Bimonthly Student Leadership Team meetings
   b. Sunday morning and Wednesday night events
   c. All activities, camps, and special events

3. Must be an example in Christian conduct and character. This involves striving for excellence in
   a. Devotional life
   b. Friendships
   c. Schoolwork
   d. Home life

4. Must be able to serve until _____

Schedule

_____ Meeting 1

_____ Student Leadership Team

_____ Student Leadership Team

_____ Student Leadership Team

_____ Student Leadership Team

_____ Student Leadership Team

_____ Student Leadership Team

_____ Christmas Banquet

Student Action Leadership Team
High School Servant-Leader Application

Name _____   School _____

Address _____   Grade: ☐ 9 ☐ 10 ☐ 11 ☐ 12

_____   Phone _____

1. How long have you been a Christian?

2. State briefly how you became a Christian and what has caused the most growth in your Christian life (use the back of this sheet.)

3. How long have you consistently attended our church?

4. What services do you regularly attend?
   ☐ Sunday morning ☐ Sunday night
   ☐ Wednesday night youth meeting
   ☐ Discipleship group/S.A.L.T.

5. Why would you like to be a high school servant-leader, and what can you contribute to this ministry?

6. What are your previous experiences working as a leader?

7. What other activities will you be involved in this year (sports, clubs, cheerleading, and so on)?

8. What does the concept "servant-leader" mean to you?

   Are you willing to be this type of leader?
   ☐ Yes ☐ No

9. Who have been the three most influential people in your life and why?

10. What do you feel are your spiritual gifts?

    How can you use them in the group this year?

11. What do you see as your strengths?

12. What do you see as your weaknesses?

Have you read the leadership team responsibility sheet? Are you willing to commit to these responsibilities for the entire year? ☐ Yes ☐ No

Signature _____

For Parents:
Have you read the leadership team responsibility sheet? Do you consent to your teenager working as a high school leadership team member? ☐ Yes ☐ No

Signature _____

Student Action Leadership Team
High School Student Leadership Team Reference Sheet

Reference sheets must be completed by each of the three people listed below.
• A high schooler within the youth group
• A teacher, coach, boss, or other influential leader in your life
• One of your parents

Applicant's Name:_____ Phone:_____

Your relationship to the student_____ How long have you known him/her?_____

1. What would you say are this student's strengths?

2. What would you say are this student's weaknesses?

3. In what ways do you feel this student has leadership potential?

4. Do you recommend him or her
   ☐ with enthusiasm
   ☐ with few reservations
   ☐ with reservations
   ☐ not sure they are ready for this type of challenge this year

Thanks for your time and input. Please return this to the student in a sealed envelope.

Student Action Leadership Team
Ministry Team Job Descriptions

1. Welcome Team
a. Welcome people on Wednesday night by saying "Hi" and talking with them.
b. Distribute name tags for people on selected Wednesday nights.
c. Do anything else that helps people feel at home.

2. Follow-up Team
a. Get visitor cards and make sure that all new people are reinvited and transportation is arranged within one week.
b. Keep a list of all new people and track their progress toward becoming active members.
c. Organize a new people's dinner.

3. Scenic Engineering Team
a. Set up for events.
b. Clean up after events and have a staff person lock up.
c. Help organize transportation for events.

4. Decorating/Refreshments Team
a. Organize refreshments for selected events.
b. Decorate rooms with posters, plants, and pictures to make the area attractive and comfortable for high school events—be creative!
c. Bring food for birthday celebrations (work with Telephone Contact/Care Team).

5. Mission Team
a. Help plan and publicize our mission trips.
b. Organize local mission efforts.
c. Plan mission reports to let us know what God is doing around the world.
d. Collect offerings to be used for supporting hunger projects.

6. Photography/Media Team
a. Organize, mark, and store all slides.
b. Organize slide and media shows for each Wednesday night. (This lets people see what God is doing and helps people get involved.)
c. Put up at least two bulletin boards and fill them with up-to-date pictures and flyers.
d. Make sure slides and pictures are taken of *all* our people, not just the popular or photogenic ones. Everyone is important in God's family!

7. Telephone Contact/Care Team
a. Call new or fringe people and invite them to events. (If they don't know about an activity, they will not come and we will not reach them for Christ.)
b. Work in conjunction with Follow-up Team when necessary.
c. Promote birthday celebrations.
d. Whenever possible, work as a team in the church office when telephoning.
e. Spread the word of our get-togethers.

8. Evangelism/Publicity Team
a. Mail a monthly newsletter/calendar (school newspaper style).
b. Plan creative ways to publicize evangelism events.
c. Advertise through any media.

9. Christian Education Team
a. Help start and promote four morning Bible studies, each in a different area.
b. Support and help run Sunday school.

10. Fund-raising Team
a. Organize "Project Serve" (our annual one-day service event).
b. Collect Sunday school offerings. Work with the Mission Team.
c. Organize other fund-raising events as needed.

11. Activities Team
a. Plan and promote youth activities.
b. Publicize the activities.

12. Area Directors Team (Team members must be juniors or seniors)
a. Know and care about all the students coming from your area.
b. Help arrange rides, invitations, and scholarships.

Student Action Leadership Team
Leadership Involvement Application Survey

"For even the Son of Man did not come to be served, but to serve, and to give his life as a ransom for many."
Mark 10:45

Name _____

First Choice:
I would like to serve on the _____ Team.
Reason:

Second Choice
I would like to serve on the _____ Team.
Reason:

People I would recommend for the following teams are:

1. Welcome Team

    Leader _____

    a. _____

    b. _____

2. Follow-up Team

    Leader _____

    a. _____

    b. _____

3. Scenic Engineering Team

    Leader _____

    a. _____

    b. _____

4. Decorating/Refreshments Team

    Leader _____

    a. _____

    b. _____

5. Mission Team

    Leader _____

    a. _____

    b. _____

6. Photography/Media Team

    Leader _____

    a. _____

    b. _____

7. Telephone Contact/Care Team

    Leader _____

    a. _____

    b. _____

8. Evangelism/Publicity Team

    Leader _____

    a. _____

    b. _____

9. Christian Education Team

    Leader _____

    a. _____

    b. _____

10. Fund-raising Team

    Leader _____

    a. _____

    b. _____

11. Activities Team

    Leader _____

    a. _____

    b. _____

12. Area Directors Team

    Leader _____

    a. _____

    b. _____

Student Action Leadership Team
Leadership Retreat Registration Form

Place:_____

Date:_____

Time:
We will leave the church at _____

and will return at _____.

Cost: $ _____to cover food,
transportation, and lodging.

You will need to bring money for _____.

What will be happening:
This will be a great time of learning, studying, getting to
know your Bible better, making new friends, and being
in on the ground floor of what God is doing in our
youth ministry.

Who may attend:
This is open to all senior highers who are
on the leadership team.

Please bring the following items in one
small suitcase: Warm clothes, tennis shoes,
Bible, notebook, pen, towel, and sleeping
bag. Please leave all stereos, washing
machines, and bad attitudes at home.

Also, please be on time—it is a long walk!

Registration fee is $ _____
(nonrefundable). The balance is due prior
to the retreat.

See you there!

Registration Form
S.A.L.T. Kickoff Retreat!

Name_____

Address _____

City/Zip_____

Phone _____

School_____

Grade: ☐ 9 ☐ 10 ☐ 11 ☐ 12

Parents: please sign below authorizing emergency treatment for your child in event of injury or illness if you are
not immediately available.

_____

SELECT: Recruiting and Selecting Student Leaders

MY FIRST ATTEMPT AT RECRUITING and selecting a leadership team was a disaster. I wanted a lot of kids to join so I made it sound like a great deal. "Be a leader—no commitment required," was the tone I unwittingly set. I emphasized the enjoyable parts and minimized the requirements. Students flocked onto the team, signed the commitment forms, and then proceeded to miss most of the meetings. They did the assignments if they felt like it, and the whole process looked a lot like Laurel and Hardy organizing a leadership experience. As I surveyed the ruins, I realized the importance of the recruitment-selection process.

How students enter the leadership team will set the tone for the quality, commitment, and performance of the leadership team. Ask any corporate executive, marriage counselor, or developer of leaders and most will agree that the selection process is a significant determining factor in the success of a business, marriage, or leadership team. Ministry teams that begin in a haphazard fashion and recruit people to half-hearted commitment usually get off the ground fast and fall even faster. The youth worker is then demoralized by the lack of commitment from the students and the students are discouraged by both their own failures and the disorganization of the program. The first step in the selection process is to be aware of three common but unhealthy strategies for selecting student leaders.

One selection process commonly used is *voting by peers*. This often turns the selection process into a popularity contest, and the student leader is elected on the basis of looks, age, status, athletic ability, or personality. Unfortunately, this process reinforces the feelings of insecurity and inferiority shared by most teenagers while failing to take into account the character of the students. Students who would make outstanding student leaders often pass up this type of leadership opportunity out of fear or insecurity. My most recent student leadership team doubled when we dispensed with the voting method of selection

81

Selection by the youth worker, another common method, is a surefire way to shorten the tenure (and maybe the life span) of the youth worker. Selection is usually followed by accusations of favoritism from the students and frustration and strained relationships with parents whose own kids weren't selected.

A third selection strategy often suggested is to *take the rowdy, rebellious students in the youth group and put them in charge*. My first year in youth ministry, we had some kids in our group who probably would have been more at home in jail. A number of people suggested to me that the best way to handle the situation would be to put these kids in charge. This would, the thinking goes, motivate these students to straighten up, fly right, and begin to imitate Mother Teresa or Billy Graham. As I implemented the strategy, I discovered that all it accomplished was to communicate to the majority of the students in our group that the way to get ahead was to be rowdy and rebellious. Most youth ministries, mine included, don't need more reinforcement of that behavior.

Here, instead, are some practical steps to take when recruiting and selecting leaders.

Invest time in prayer. It may be more than coincidence that Jesus spent an entire night in prayer prior to calling the disciples to form a ministry team. As we take time for prayer and reflection, we gain new insight into students as well as direction for the ministry team.

Recruit support and advice. The success of our programs will be greatly helped by support from key people. Encouragement and support from the senior pastor and the church board will give the program priority and visibility. It is essential to include the church's leaders in the planning process of formulating the leadership team. They may give valuable insight and wisdom. People are often more supportive of that which they help create.

Also, if the parents are informed and "on board," the students will be more consistent. A small amount of time spent gathering information, advice, and support will make your leadership program larger and more effective.

The following form can be photocopied and passed out or used in an interview format.

Student Action Leadership Team
Brainstorming and Planning

1. What needs for leadership development do you see in our youths?

2. Which students do you think are ready for involvement in a ministry team?

3. Which students do you think would be easy to overlook in the process of recruiting?

4. What meeting times would be best for your son or daughter? (Give several options.)

5. In which areas of our church would you like to see these students take on responsibility?

6. Would you be willing to look over this program design and make suggestions?

Take stock of which students are ready to be challenged to leader-ship. Evaluation is a critical part of the selection process. Not all students in the youth group are at the same place in terms of Christian commitment, spiritual maturity, or readiness to participate in leadership. A key to recruiting and selecting leaders is to identify and *work with* those who are ready for commitment, dedication, and development, while *working at* developing readiness in those who may be leaders in the future. The following worksheet is designed to help the youth worker identify students who may be ready for involvement in student leadership.

Student Action Leadership Team
Evaluation Planning Page

Names of students who are DEFINITELY READY—Write down the names of the students who are ready for involvement in discipleship and leadership:

What are my plans for motivating these students to involvement?

Names of students who are CLOSE TO BEING READY Write down the names of the students who are growing and are close to being ready for involvement in leadership:

What are my plans for enabling and encouraging these students to grow in commitment to the leadership team?

Implement your selection process. To begin, form a selection committee with two other people that interviews the students who apply and informs them of their selection and ministry leadership responsibilities. This will ease the pressure on you, give added wisdom to the process, and help eliminate complaints of favoritism. Turning a student down for the team is always painful for both the student and the committee. You may be able to alleviate the need for this by setting a sober tone and calling for serious commitment. The very process of filling out application forms will weed out many borderline students. Because of the seriousness of our application process, we rarely had to turn down a student.

When the selection committee is ready, announce the new program in all youth group meetings for two consecutive weeks. Hand out the Student Leadership Application Packet to all interested students. Invite students and parents to an informational meeting, held at the same time your leadership meetings will take place.

During the two weeks the students are deciding whether or not to apply, encourage those you have identified as ready for involvement in this type of ministry challenge. Some of the best potential leaders may be insecure or unsure of their abilities to contribute. When we were putting together our first student leadership team, I noticed that Lisa had not signed on to be part of it. She was easily one of the brightest and most helpful students I had ever met, yet she did not feel like a "leader." She wanted to join but thought this was for "up-front" types only. I explained that we would love to have her; during the next three years, she was one of our best servant-leaders. A little encouragement to these students can go a long way.

The informational meeting, above all else, should set a positive tone of commitment for the leadership team. Because the purpose is to give information, it is usually most effective to invite both teenagers and parents.

At the meeting, explain the goals of the leadership team and the commitment required regarding meetings, assignments, and responsibilities. Explain how the application process works, and set up interview times for students who are interested. If you are limiting the size of the leadership team, explain your priorities for selection. For example, seniors may have first priority. The following is a sample agenda for an informational meeting.

S.A.L.T.—Student Action Leadership Team
Informational Meeting Schedule

Setup

Create an upbeat atmosphere: Play music and have refreshments available.

Welcome and Prayer

Leadership Program Explanation

1. Pass out materials.

2. Have a student from a past program share what the program means.

3. Cover the program goals, requirements, meetings, and retreat.

4. Explain how the application process works.

Close

1. Thank people for coming.

2. Let students sign up for interview times.

3. Close in prayer.

Finally, the selection committee should inform the students as soon as possible of its decisions. This should be done in person by the youth pastor and can be used as a motivational time for growth. In most of the leadership application processes in which I have been involved, we have accepted every student who applied. For many students, this type of process enables them to rethink and reorder their priorities around spiritual growth and meaningful service. From Moses to the disciples, the call to dedication, discipleship, and involvement in leadership has been a life-changing experience. Once you have selected the leadership team, the training (and the fun) begins.

TRAIN: A Five-Week Training Course for Student Leaders

NOW THAT YOUR STUDENT LEADERSHIP team is on board, it's time to train. The most natural place for training will be at the weekly or biweekly leadership team meeting. This chapter contains a five-week training course designed to achieve four goals.

1. To provide encouragement by *creating team unity*.

2. To develop competence by *teaching ministry skills*.

3. To give ownership by *allowing time for planning*.

4. To create responsibility through *reporting and accountability*.

Each week's meeting includes the following basic format:

COMPONENT 1. Team Building (see the ideas in Appendix A).

COMPONENT 2. Content (discipleship and skill training).

COMPONENT 3. Planning (for individuals and the youth ministry as a whole).

COMPONENT 4. Reporting and Prayer (reporting on areas of responsibility).

Because many of the students may experience uncertainty or limited success, all of the above should include liberal amounts of affirmation, encouragement, and prayer.

A sample schedule for a weekly meeting might look like the following:

S.A.L.T.—Student Action Leadership Team
Sunday Night Schedule

6:00-6:05 **Welcome and Prayer**

6:05-6:25 **Team Building** (Relational games, sharing, prayer, and so on—see Appendix A)

6:25-6:50 **Content** (Bible study, training video, guest speaker, discipleship, or leadership training—see Appendix C)

6:50-7:05 **Planning** (Working on their own areas or together working on plans for the whole group)

7:05-7:15 **Reporting and Prayer** (Sharing of plans, encouragement, affirmation, and prayer)

The following pages are a complete five-week training course based on this planning model.

Your First Five Weeks
of Leadership Development
Five Complete Leadership Meetings

THEMES FOR THE FIVE MEETINGS

WEEK 1—*Making an Impact by Learning to Care I*

WEEK 2—*Making an Impact by Learning to Care II*

WEEK 3—*Learning to Lead by Learning to Serve*

WEEK 4—*Discovering and Developing Your Spiritual Gifts I*

WEEK 5—*Discovering and Developing Your Spiritual Gifts II*

S.A.L.T.—Student Action Leadership Team
WEEK 1—*Making an Impact*
by Learning to Care I

GOALS AND OBJECTIVES

1. Students will enjoy the first leadership meeting and begin to take the program seriously.

2. Students will begin to sense the importance of being involved in ministry.

3. The team members will feel supported by praying for each other's ministry assignments at the end of the meeting.

COMPONENT 1—TEAM BUILDING
- Welcome students and have one of them open in prayer.
- Play "Common Ground" (see Appendix A).

COMPONENT 2—CONTENT
- Introduce the theme for the next two weeks by reading the following: In the U.S. today, within the next thirty minutes,

  29 kids will attempt suicide

  22 teenage girls will get abortions

  685 teenagers will begin to use some form of narcotics

  228 kids will be sexually or physically abused at home

  (**Source**: Rich van Pelt, "How to Help Your Friends in Trouble," Grow For It Tour, 1989.)

The world needs a group of students who learn to lead by learning to care.

- Pass out copies of "The Lifesaving Station" (see Appendix C) and have students read in groups of twos. Spend some time working through the questions and point out the critical importance of a church youth ministry made up of individuals who care.
- Announce that the assignment for the next week is to be involved in the "Youth Group Scouts" activity described in Chapter Five.

  This adventure is designed to show teenagers how a new person feels upon entering a youth group.

COMPONENT 3—PLANNING
- Give the students fifteen minutes to plan their areas of responsibility and allow them to plan as a whole group, whenever necessary.

COMPONENT 4—REPORTING AND PRAYER
- Have the students share their plans with the group, and pray for each other's ministries.

- Put the students in groups of two and make arrangements for the "Scouts" activity.
- Close by passing out Student Study Sheet #1 (see Appendix F) and reminding the student leaders that the study needs to be done before the next meeting. (You may want to meet with several of the students and work on this together to get them off to a running start. Starting right is half the battle.)

S.A.L.T.—Student Action Leadership Team
WEEK 2—*Making an Impact*
by Learning to Care II

GOALS AND OBJECTIVES

1. Students will continue to discover and apply their commitment to care.

2. Students will be highly involved in an active meeting.

COMPONENT 1—TEAM BUILDING

- As a group, do the "Life Auction" exercise (see Appendix C). You may want to use play money for the game. This is a great game that allows people to cut to the issues of priority and importance.

COMPONENT 2—CONTENT

- Pair up students and have them share the insights they have gained from visiting other churches. Focus first on sharing experiences and then on sharing feelings.

- As a group, debrief the experiences. Focus on how it feels to be an outsider. Brainstorm ways to make people feel welcome in your own ministry. You may want to have each student choose a person he or she thinks needs friendship. Have the kids write out specific ways they will be friends to these people in the coming week.

COMPONENT 3—PLANNING

- Have the group do whole group planning first, then break into ministry teams for planning.

COMPONENT 4—REPORTING AND PRAYER

- Let the group members share personal prayer requests (you may need to kick this off), then have them share their ministry plans.
- Close by having the students share their observations from Student Study Sheet #1. Then pass out Student Study Sheet #2 (see Appendix F) as the assignment for next week.

Personal Assignment for the Group Leader. Do the "Unwanted Guest" exercise (see Appendix C) and arrange for that person to come to the Week 4 leadership meeting to share his or her observations.

S.A.L.T.—Student Action Leadership Team
WEEK 3—*Learning to Lead by Learning to Serve*

GOALS AND OBJECTIVES

1. Students will begin to gain a clear view of their God-given strengths and will begin to decide to use those strengths to serve.
2. Students will affirm each other.

COMPONENT 1—TEAM BUILDING

- Begin with the whole group sharing observations from Student Study Sheet #2.
- Do the "Strength Voting" exercise described in Chapter Five of this book. This is an excellent way to enable students to discover their strengths in the context of encouragement. Point out at the end that our strengths and abilities may be God's indication of a direction for service.

COMPONENT 2—CONTENT

- Pass out the two TalkSheets on Servanthood (pp. 95, 96). Allow the students a few minutes to complete them, then have the teenagers share their answers. This is an excellent tool for looking at biblical principles of service and enabling students to take serving seriously.

COMPONENT 3—PLANNING

- Give the students fifteen minutes to plan their areas of leadership.

COMPONENT 4—REPORTING AND PRAYER

- Close by pointing out how the students' strengths are being used in their areas of ministry. End with prayers of thanksgiving for each other.

- Pass out Student Study Sheet #3 (see Appendix F) as the assignment for the next meeting.

Servanthood

1

The Bible gives us a variety of ways to serve each other in the body of Christ. Listed below are a few examples. Next to each one, put a symbol to indicate your feelings:

★ = I do pretty well with this one.

N = No, I never do this one.

➚ = I need God to help me with this one.

? = I don't understand this one.

♥ = Someone in this group has done this for me.

S = This is our group's greatest strength.

W = This is our group's greatest weakness.

We are to . . .

_____ Pray for each other (Ephesians 6:18-19).

_____ Share our possessions with one another (Deuteronomy 15:7; Romans 12:13).

_____ Confess our sins to each other (James 5:16).

_____ Forgive each other (Colossians 3:12-13).

_____ Discipline each other (Galatians 6:1-2; Matthew 18:15; 2 Thessalonians 3:14-15).

_____ Bear each other's burdens (Galatians 6:2; Romans 15:1).

_____ Be kind to each other (Romans 14:19; 1 Thessalonians 5:11).

_____ Greet one another (Romans 16:16; 1 Corinthians 16:20; 2 Corinthians 13:12).

_____ Accept one another (Romans 15:7; 14:1).

_____ Show hospitality to each other (1 Peter 4:7-10).

_____ Teach one another (Colossians 3:16).

2

List three ways you could serve others in your church or youth group:

1.

2.

3.

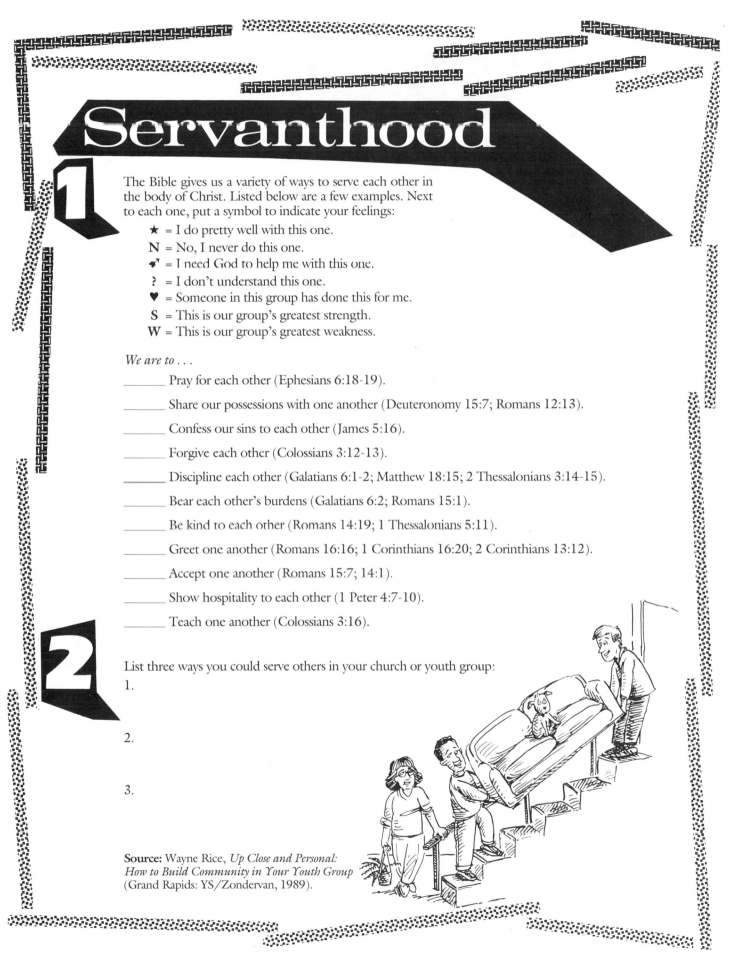

Source: Wayne Rice, *Up Close and Personal: How to Build Community in Your Youth Group* (Grand Rapids: YS/Zondervan, 1989).

Servanthood

1 *Read John 13:1-9, 12-17,* then answer the questions below.

Why did Jesus wash the disciples' feet?

Why didn't Peter want Jesus to wash his feet?

What might be the equivalent to washing someone's feet today?

Can you think of a time when someone "washed your feet"?

2 *Read Philippians 2:1-11.* Verses 7 and 8 give us two keys to servanthood—humility and sacrificial love.

How do you define these two concepts? Read the statements below and check whether you agree or disagree.

	AGREE	DISAGREE
A humble person		
Tries to "out-humble" everyone else	☐	☐
Tries to follow the Golden Rule	☐	☐
Always goes last in everything	☐	☐
Never brags	☐	☐
Has a low self-image	☐	☐
Should not try to attain success	☐	☐
Deliberately loses so the other person can win	☐	☐
Puts others first; themselves second	☐	☐
Has no rights to speak of	☐	☐
Gets pushed around a lot	☐	☐
Is motivated by love	☐	☐
Sacrificial love is		
Not very practical nowadays	☐	☐
Giving up something for someone else's good	☐	☐
Painful and costly	☐	☐
Having a martyr complex	☐	☐
The highest form of love there is	☐	☐
Usually unnecessary	☐	☐
Awesome	☐	☐
How all Christians should treat each other	☐	☐
Self-denial	☐	☐
Dying for somebody	☐	☐
Doing whatever is required on behalf of someone	☐	☐

Source: Wayne Rice, *Up Close and Personal: How to Build Community in Your Youth Group* (Grand Rapids: YS/Zondervan, 1989).

S.A.L.T.—Student Action Leadership Team
WEEK 4—*Discovering and Developing Your Spiritual Gifts I*

GOALS AND OBJECTIVES

1. Team members will begin to get an idea of what spiritual gifts are.

2. Students will begin the process of discovering their gifts.

COMPONENT 1—TEAM BUILDING

- Have the students form small groups and share two or three applications from Student Study Sheet #3.

- Introduce the "Unwanted Guest" and have that person share all observations about her or his visit to the youth group. Take ten to fifteen minutes to talk as a group about ways to take action on the results of the discussion.

COMPONENT 2—CONTENT

- Pass out the worksheet "Spiritual Gifts: What Do They Mean?" (p. 98) and allow the students to work in pairs. Have the students talk as a whole group and define possible uses for each gift.

- Pass out the second "Spiritual Gifts" worksheet (p. 99) and have the students rate themselves. Have each student share his or her high scores.

COMPONENT 3—PLANNING

- Give the students time to plan for their areas of responsibility.

COMPONENT 4—REPORTING AND PRAYER

- Allow the kids to share their plans and do any whole group planning. Take time to pray for their ministries.

- Pass out Student Study Sheet #4 (see Appendix F) and remind the students that this is due next week.

Spiritual Gifts

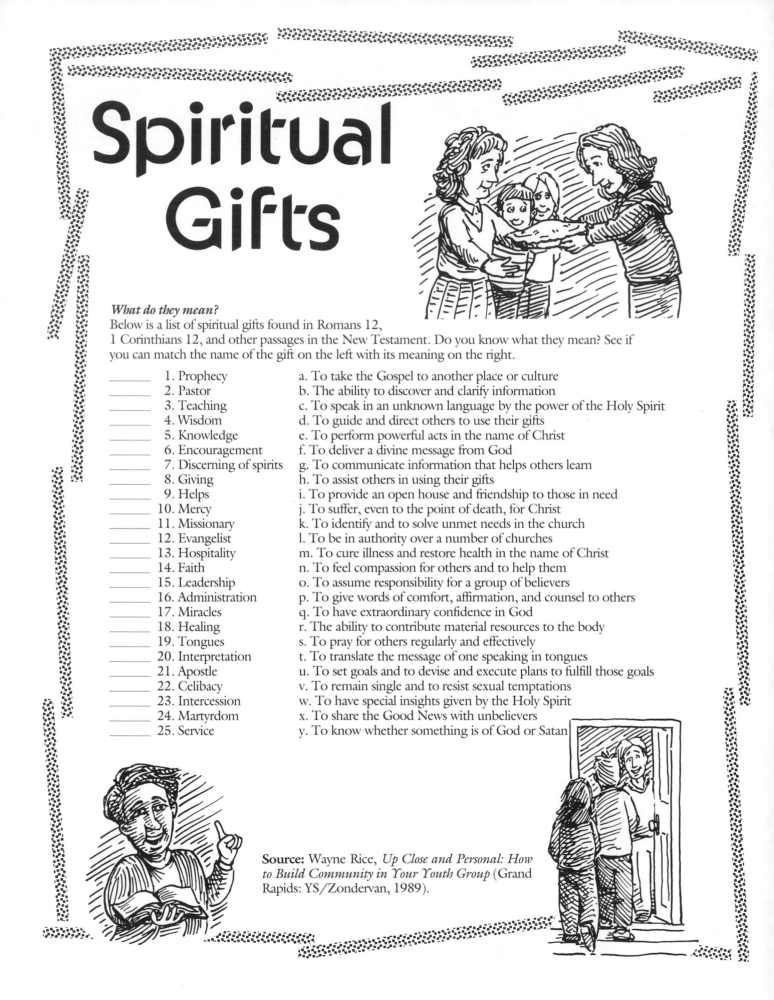

What do they mean?

Below is a list of spiritual gifts found in Romans 12, 1 Corinthians 12, and other passages in the New Testament. Do you know what they mean? See if you can match the name of the gift on the left with its meaning on the right.

_____	1. Prophecy	a. To take the Gospel to another place or culture
_____	2. Pastor	b. The ability to discover and clarify information
_____	3. Teaching	c. To speak in an unknown language by the power of the Holy Spirit
_____	4. Wisdom	d. To guide and direct others to use their gifts
_____	5. Knowledge	e. To perform powerful acts in the name of Christ
_____	6. Encouragement	f. To deliver a divine message from God
_____	7. Discerning of spirits	g. To communicate information that helps others learn
_____	8. Giving	h. To assist others in using their gifts
_____	9. Helps	i. To provide an open house and friendship to those in need
_____	10. Mercy	j. To suffer, even to the point of death, for Christ
_____	11. Missionary	k. To identify and to solve unmet needs in the church
_____	12. Evangelist	l. To be in authority over a number of churches
_____	13. Hospitality	m. To cure illness and restore health in the name of Christ
_____	14. Faith	n. To feel compassion for others and to help them
_____	15. Leadership	o. To assume responsibility for a group of believers
_____	16. Administration	p. To give words of comfort, affirmation, and counsel to others
_____	17. Miracles	q. To have extraordinary confidence in God
_____	18. Healing	r. The ability to contribute material resources to the body
_____	19. Tongues	s. To pray for others regularly and effectively
_____	20. Interpretation	t. To translate the message of one speaking in tongues
_____	21. Apostle	u. To set goals and to devise and execute plans to fulfill those goals
_____	22. Celibacy	v. To remain single and to resist sexual temptations
_____	23. Intercession	w. To have special insights given by the Holy Spirit
_____	24. Martyrdom	x. To share the Good News with unbelievers
_____	25. Service	y. To know whether something is of God or Satan

Source: Wayne Rice, _Up Close and Personal: How to Build Community in Your Youth Group_ (Grand Rapids: YS/Zondervan, 1989).

Spiritual Gifts

Do you know what your spiritual gift is? (You may have been given more than one!) For each of the nine listed below, circle a number to indicate whether you feel weak or strong in any of them.

The Gift of Service
God has given me a special ability for helping out whenever a need arises. If there is a job that needs to be done, I am willing to do it if I can.

1 2 3 4 5 6 7 8 9 10
Weak   Strong

The Gift of Teaching
God has given me a skill for helping others to learn. I am good at motivating people to learn and grow in the Christian faith.

1 2 3 4 5 6 7 8 9 10
Weak   Strong

The Gift of Speaking God's Truth (Evangelism)
God has given me a gift for communicating the Gospel to others. When I explain the Good News, God seems to use my words to bring insight and understanding about his grace.

1 2 3 4 5 6 7 8 9 10
Weak   Strong

The Gift of Encouragement
God has given me the ability to see the best in others. I find it easy to compliment people and to point out their strengths.

1 2 3 4 5 6 7 8 9 10
Weak   Strong

The Gift of Leadership
God has given me a gift for organization. I can get things done. I find it easy to take responsibility and direct others.

1 2 3 4 5 6 7 8 9 10
Weak   Strong

The Gift of Kindness (Mercy)
God has given me the ability to be compassionate and understanding whenever someone is in trouble or needs help. I enjoy being able to minister to someone who is feeling down.

1 2 3 4 5 6 7 8 9 10
Weak   Strong

The Gift of Generosity (Giving)
God has given me a freedom to share myself with others. I find it easy to give whatever I can to others or to God's work whenever a special need arises.

1 2 3 4 5 6 7 8 9 10
Weak   Strong

The Gift of Faith
God has given me complete confidence and trust in him. Whenever I pray, I believe and fully expect that God will answer my prayer.

1 2 3 4 5 6 7 8 9 10
Weak   Strong

The Gift of Helps
God has given me the desire and ability to assist other members of the body to use their spiritual gifts. I enjoy helping other people to be more effective in their ministries.

1 2 3 4 5 6 7 8 9 10
Weak   Strong

Source: Wayne Rice, *Up Close and Personal: How to Build Community in Your Youth Group* (Grand Rapids: YS/Zondervan, 1989).

S.A.L.T.—Student Action Leadership Team
WEEK 5—*Discovering and Developing Your Spiritual Gifts II*

GOALS AND OBJECTIVES

1. Team members will take steps to identify their gifts for ministry.

2. Team members will list ways to begin to use their gifts in leadership.

3. Team members will feel supported by praying for each other's ministry assignments at the end of the meeting.

COMPONENT 1—TEAM BUILDING

- Play "Gift Guessing" (see Appendix C) as students arrive. This will require some preparation. You may want to give the leadership of this game to one or two students.

COMPONENT 2—CONTENT

- Begin with the whole group discussing Student Study Sheet #4.

- Pass out copies of Appendix G, "Discover Your Spiritual Gifts! (Teen Edition)," and have the students take the test in class. Review and discuss their answers and scores. Then have each student list his or her top three gifts on blank sheets of paper. Pass the sheets around the room and have the students list ways they have seen each others' gifts at work. Allow one minute per person. If there is time, have the students list one specific way they would like to use their gifts in service.

COMPONENT 3—PLANNING

- Allow the students time to work on their areas, then give them time as a whole group for planning significant upcoming events.

COMPONENT 4—REPORTING AND PRAYER

- Close by having students share prayer requests for their areas of responsibility and pray for each other.

The following form is designed to help you to plan your own leadership meetings using the resources in Appendixes A, B, and C.

Student Action Leadership Team
Weekly Meeting Planning Worksheet

GOALS—My objectives for this meeting are:

PROGRAM—My plan for the elements of the meeting's program is:

COMPONENT 1—TEAM BUILDING: What will we do during the meeting to build unity?

COMPONENT 2—CONTENT: What material will we cover during the meeting?

COMPONENT 3—PLANNING:

1. Do the students need time or input for planning their own areas of responsibility? If so, how will this be structured?

2. Does the leadership team need time to plan upcoming events or activities for the youth group? If so, what plans and what decisions need to be made?

COMPONENT 4—REPORTING AND PRAYER:

1. Who needs to make reports on progress or upcoming plans?

2. How can we affirm and encourage these people for their progress?

3. Potential areas for training:

Close the planning time with prayer.

DELEGATE: Developing Responsibility and Accountability

NOW WE MOVE TO THE most critical and challenging area of leadership development—the delegation of responsibility. Delegation is critical because it is almost impossible for an individual to develop maturity, competence, or leadership ability apart from responsibility. Giving teenagers significant responsibility develops these qualities.

Delegation is challenging. If the ball is not handed off properly, it can easily be dropped, and then programs suffer, demoralized students feel like failures, and already burned-out youth workers become even busier as they mutter, "If you want something done right, do it yourself."

This chapter will provide a developmental process for successful delegation and then focus on strategies and resources for developing responsibility in three key areas of student leadership.

Successful delegation is not a one-step process. Many youth workers have found these four steps helpful in summarizing the process of delegation.

STEP 1. I do it (preparation). I must have knowledge of what I am about to communicate. Personal competence will lead to the ability to communicate that knowledge to others.

STEP 2. I do it and you watch (partnership). The training process has begun. The potential leader is gaining knowledge by observation.

STEP 3. You do it and I watch (coaching). The shift has occurred. The responsibility has shifted into the hands of the trainee and I am now in the position of an encouraging observer. The key at this phase is to have the patience to avoid rescuing potential failures and to provide encouragement and feedback.

103

STEP 4. **You do it** (delegation). The process of training has now reached the delegation point. The odds of success are much higher *because* of the training.

With the process of delegation in mind, let's consider youth workers helping students developmentally by delegating responsibility in three major areas.

Give students responsibility for decision making. Delegating decision making responsibility to the student leaders generates both ownership and maturity. Maturity occurs when people begin to grapple with decisions, direction, and consequences. Because many of the decisions regarding the lives of teenagers are made by adults, most contemporary students are not learning the skill of decision making. Life is a matter of priorities and commitments and the development of decision-making skills is critical for developing those characteristics.

Students can be given responsibility for setting the goals and planning the programs of the youth group. The following resources are designed to help the students take ownership of the youth ministry.

Youth Group Planning Survey

The Youth Group Planning Survey helps the student leaders plan the major areas of the youth ministry.

Youth Group Planning Survey

Topics

Circle the ten that most interest you.

1. Alcohol
2. Anger
3. Bible studies
4. Competition
5. Careers
6. Colleges
7. Dating
8. Death
9. Drugs
10. Ecology
11. Faith
12. Getting along with brothers/sisters
13. Getting along with parents
14. Getting along with friends
15. Getting along with adults
16. God's will
17. Group pressure
18. World hunger
19. Identity
20. Independence
21. Jealousy
22. Love
23. Marriage
24. Poverty/affluence
25. Religion
26. Race
27. Sex
28. School
29. Suburbia
30. Women's liberation
31. World religions
32. Values
Others:
33.
34.
35.

Methods

Circle the four that you most enjoy.

1. Skits
2. Puppets
3. Making banners
4. Discussion
5. Rapping
6. Panel
7. Movies
8. Filmstrips
9. Role-playing
10. Speakers
11. Group study
12. Workbooks
Others:
13.
14.
15.

Recreation

Circle the eight that you most enjoy.

1. Beach
2. City park
3. Skiing
4. Softball
5. Volleyball
6. Kickball
7. Over-the-line
8. Bike hike
9. Swimming
10. Progressive dinner
11. Pizza party
12. Horseback riding
13. Miniature golf
14. Tubing
15. Go-carts
16. Bowling
17. Trampolines
18. Roller skating
19. Ice skating
20. Dance/disco
21. Cookout
22. Hayride
23. Square dancing
24. Canoeing
Others:
25.
26.
27.

Service Projects

Circle the six that you most want to do.

1. Fix up youth room
2. Christmas caroling
3. Trick-or-treat for UNICEF
4. Spook house for UNICEF
5. Car wash for world hunger
6. Visit nursing home
7. Thanksgiving baskets
8. Tour a United Fund agency
9. Collect aluminum cans
10. Newspaper drive
11. Visit prospective church members
12. Cook meal for congregation to raise money for retreats
13. Sponsor drop in center for neighborhood youth
14. Adopt an orphan overseas
Others:
15.
16.
17.

(**Source:** Wayne Rice, ed., *Ideas 25-28* [El Cajon, Calif.: Youth Specialties, 1980-1985], 160.)

LEADERSHIP EVENT PLANNING SHEET

Most youth ministries have a weekly meeting that is planned and pulled off by adults. This generates ownership and commitment on the part of the adults, who are usually frustrated by the inconsistent attendance and lack of commitment on the part of the students. The adults are more committed because they feel responsible for the program. The key to generating consistency and commitment on the part of the students is to give them the responsibility for planning the program. This planning sheet will give students maximum ownership while providing them with structure for the planning of a typical series of meetings.

Leadership Event Planning Sheet
Wednesday Night Planning

Date	Event/Game	Speaker/Theme	Group	Time	Suggestions
9/25			Staff		Pizza Bash
10/1			Staff		Pizza Bash
10/8			Staff		Volleyball Variations
10/9			Staff		
10/15			Staff		Football Fever
10/22			Staff		Camfel (see Appendix E)
10/29			Staff		Halloween Costumes
11/5			Staff		Volleyball
11/12			Staff		Commitment
11/19			Staff		Bible True/False
11/26			Staff		
12/3			Staff		Guys' Baking Contest

ROTATING PLANNING SESSION

Here's a great way to add a little excitement and enthusiasm to planning with large groups. Divide your entire group into teams of four.

Place tables around the room and assign each of the tables a brainstorm topic, such as recreation ideas, fund-raising projects, discussion topics, and service projects. Each group sits at one of the tables with pencil and paper. At the sound of a buzzer or whistle, each group has just five minutes to write down as many ideas as it can. When the whistle sounds again, each group moves to another table in a clockwise direction and writes ideas on the new topic.

To add to the fun, challenge the groups to see which group can think of the most ideas for any one topic and then award prizes. At the conclusion of this planning game, you'll find that you have tons of ideas and that the boring planning session wasn't so boring after all.

EVENT RESPONSE SHEET

Another way to develop responsibility is evaluation. Evaluation by the youth group will lead to steady improvement in the students' leadership efforts. The Event Response Sheet is an evaluation tool and is a good way to enable students to evaluate the programs they are now planning and leading.

Event Response Sheet

Evaluation of project, activity, or study:_____

Date _____

Grade in School: ☐ 9 ☐ 10 ☐ 11 ☐ 12

Sex: ☐ M ☐ F

Scoring key

90-100	Strongly agree or Yes!
80-89	Mildly agree
70-79	Disagree
60-69	Strongly disagree or No!

1. Buildup—Were you aware of the event? How well were you informed? Did you have adequate time to prepare to participate in the event?

Score: _____

2. Objectives—Did you understand what was to be accomplished? Was it clear to you what was going on?

Score: _____

3. Value—Was the evening valuable? Was it worth participating in? Was it something you thought was important for students to consider?

Score: _____

4. Interest—Did it meet a need or interest that you have? Did it benefit you in your Christian growth? Was it helpful to Christian living?

Score: _____

5. Leadership—Did the leaders seem prepared? Did they present the material thoroughly? Do you think they tried to do a good job?

Score: _____

6. Repeatability—Would you recommend repeating this event again? Do you think an annual event of this type would be good?

Score: _____

Outstanding factors:

Areas to improve upon:

LEADERSHIP PLANNING RETREAT

Much of the challenge in giving students decision-making responsibility is finding the time to plan. Brainstorming and planning take time. A student planning retreat is a great way to implement the above ideas. Take the youths on a retreat at the start of the year and let them plan the yearly calendar. Have sheets prepared with brainstorming ideas for retreats, activities, socials, Sunday school, sponsor recruiting, game ideas, and so on. You may want to have the students lead the meeting. The time spent will be worth the effort.

Give teenagers the responsibility for ministry to their friends. No one understands and relates to a teenager better than another teenager. Getting students involved in ministry to their own friends is the most effective type of youth ministry. The Institute of American Church Growth released a study that demonstrates the importance of peer ministry in the evangelistic life of the church.[1] The study asked the question, "Why do people become Christians and join the church?" The answers are revealing.

Walk-in	2 percent
Program	3-4 percent
Pastor	3-5 percent
Special need	2-3 percent
Visitation	1 percent
Crusade	.001 percent
Friend/relative	70-90 percent

It is obvious that 70 to 90 percent of the growth of our youth ministries will be directly related to the way we help our students take on responsibility for reaching their friends. We can start by teaching students to pray for their friends. The Ten-Minute All-Night Prayer Meeting is a great way to introduce students to the concept of praying for their friends.

TEN-MINUTE ALL-NIGHT PRAYER MEETING

Take a group of students to various sites around your city and let them spend ten minutes praying for the people related to those locations. Go to the local high school and pray for high school students. Next the junior high, and so on. This type of prayer meeting holds the students' interest and builds community while giving students a heart for their friends.

SPECIAL EVENT CHECKLIST

Allow students to plan events and programs designed to reach their friends. They will come up with ideas their friends will like and they'll also be far more committed to bringing them in. Because most students have had little experience planning events, they may miss some (or all) of the details. The Special Event Checklist is designed to ensure that a group covers all the bases in the process of planning and leading an event.

Special Event Checklist

What's happening? _____

_____

Date(s): _____

Time(s) or Schedule: _____

_____

Alternative date(s): _____

Where? _____

_____

Special preparations: _____

_____

Special equipment: _____

_____

Who is it happening for? _____

Estimated Number: _____

Can they bring friends? ☐ Yes ☐ No

Is there is a charge? ☐ Yes ☐ No

How much? _____ per _____

To whom? _____

Profit making? ☐ Yes ☐ No

Who gets proceeds? _____

Donation? _____

How much? _____ %

Is there a registration slip and/or parental permission slip? ☐ Yes ☐ No

Who will type/write it? _____

Is number of participants limited? ☐ Yes ☐ No

If yes, number who may register: _____

Who is responsible for contacting those invited?

_____

Media? _____

By what date? _____

(L) Letter (B) Bulletin (N) Weekly Net News (P) Phone
(C) Community (PC) Postcard (M) Bulk mailing to youth
(O) Other, specify:

_____

By what date must slips and/or money be returned?

_____

Return to whom? _____

Address: _____

Make check payable to: _____

Emergency number(s): _____

_____

To be published? ☐ Yes ☐ No

Is there a fee break for early registration? ☐ Yes ☐ No

By when? _____

Refunds? ☐ Yes ☐ No

How much? _____

Any specific rules/regulations? (list) _____

_____

Transportation plans: _____

_____

Costs? _____

Who pays? _____

Organizer? _____

Should plans be in contact media? ☐ Yes ☐ No

If yes, details: _____

_____

Accommodations necessary? _____

_____

Costs? _____

Who pays? _____

Organizer? _____

Meals/food: _____

_____

Costs? _____

Who pays? _____

Organizer? _____

Special equipment participants must bring:

_____

Cleanup? _____

Who is responsible? _____

Should participants be notified to bring extra money? ☐ Yes ☐ No

Amount: _____

"Spiritual" aspects: _____

_____

Who is responsible? _____

Does event require adult chaperons? ☐ Yes ☐ No

If so, how many? _____

Who will get them? _____

By what date? _____

Which youths are directly responsible for putting this event together?

_____

_____

Do any adult official(s) have to be notified? ☐ Yes ☐ No

If yes, who? _____

Position: _____

Who will notify? _____

By what date? _____

Must any special form(s) be filled out? ☐ Yes ☐ No

If yes, which forms? _____

_____

Who will fill out? _____

By what date? _____

TELEPHONE CONTACT/CARE TEAM

We can develop our students' abilities to initiate and build friend-ships. The following idea, the Telephone Contact/Care Team, creates a phone network of students who "spread the word" quickly to their friends about an upcoming event. This will build relationships (teenagers love phones) and ensure that no one is left out of events.

Telephone Contact/Care Team

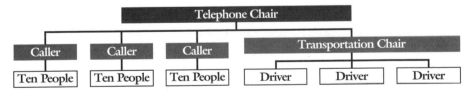

Give students responsibility for their own spiritual growth. The students who last over the long haul will be those who own their own faith. The following ideas are designed to get students involved in their own growth.

YEARLY PLANNING SURVEY

One way to give students responsibility for their spiritual lives is to have them evaluate their needs for growth and then design a program to meet those needs. The following tool gets students thinking about and evaluating where they are and where they want to go as individuals and as a group.

Yearly Planning Survey

	THIS IS ME	NOT SURE	THIS ISN'T ME
1. I have accepted Jesus as my personal Savior.	☐	☐	☐
2. I believe that the only way for a person to be happy is to know Christ.	☐	☐	☐
3. I believe that prayers are answered.	☐	☐	☐
4. I believe that it is important for Christians to witness for Christ.	☐	☐	☐
5. I know what my spiritual gifts are.	☐	☐	☐
6. I believe that the Bible is the true Word of God.	☐	☐	☐
7. I often doubt that God really exists.	☐	☐	☐
8. I believe that Jesus was a great man, but that's about it.	☐	☐	☐
9. I believe in life after death (including a literal heaven and hell).	☐	☐	☐
10. On the whole, I am satisfied with myself.	☐	☐	☐
11. I have some bad habits I'd like to get rid of.	☐	☐	☐
12. I tend to be a lonely person.	☐	☐	☐
13. People come to me for advice.	☐	☐	☐
14. I am considered popular by most people.	☐	☐	☐
15. I wish I had more respect for myself.	☐	☐	☐
16. I make good grades in school.	☐	☐	☐
17. I like to watch and participate in sports.	☐	☐	☐
18. I feel no one knows the real me.	☐	☐	☐

	THIS IS ME	NOT SURE	THIS ISN'T ME
19. My family is very important to me.	☐	☐	☐
20. My church youth group is a high priority in my life.	☐	☐	☐
21. Youth group meets many of my needs.	☐	☐	☐
22. Some of the members of the youth group are my closest friends.	☐	☐	☐
23. I think this group is too clique oriented.	☐	☐	☐
24. I often feel left out of the youth group.	☐	☐	☐
25. I think youth group needs a lot of improvement.	☐	☐	☐
26. I would like to have more fun and recreation at youth group meetings.	☐	☐	☐
27. I attend youth group primarily because my folks make me.	☐	☐	☐
28. I'd like to bring my friends to youth group.	☐	☐	☐
29. I think our youth group has good leaders.	☐	☐	☐
30. The youth group discussions and activities influence me a great deal.	☐	☐	☐
31. I have witnessed to at least one person in the last month.	☐	☐	☐
32. I am basically very selfish and don't care that much about others.	☐	☐	☐
33. I enjoy getting together with other Christians.	☐	☐	☐
34. I enjoy worshipping at church.	☐	☐	☐
35. I set aside time on a regular basis for personal devotions (Bible reading, prayer, or meditation).	☐	☐	☐
36. I like to pray with other Christians.	☐	☐	☐
37. I feel a need to grow deeper in my faith.	☐	☐	☐
38. I have led someone to Christ before.	☐	☐	☐
39. I am happy with my involvement in church.	☐	☐	☐
40. For me, living a Christian life is almost impossible most of the time.	☐	☐	☐

Strengths of our youth group:

Weaknesses of our youth group:

Please check five of the following activities that you would like to see our youth group do in the near future:

☐ Beach party
☐ Tubing party
☐ Halloween party
☐ Movie night
☐ Camping trip
☐ Host a dance
☐ Go to a concert
☐ Hayride
☐ Host a Christian concert

☐ Go to Disneyland
☐ Waterskiing trip
☐ Go to a ball game
☐ Lock-in
☐ Bowling
☐ Progressive dinner
☐ Roller skating
☐ Bike hike
☐ Weekend retreat
☐ Summer camp

☐ Youth week
☐ Youth-led worship
☐ Trip to different colleges
☐ Put on a play
☐ Service project
☐ A fund-raiser
☐ Work camp
☐ Car rally

☐ Other:_____

CONTENT SURVEY

Another great area for developing responsibility is the determination of the content for Sunday school. The following survey has been used by many youth workers to give students ownership and responsibility of the classroom time.

Content Survey

✔ the ten topics that interest you most.
★ three of the ten you would most like to learn about.

☐ Sex
☐ Lord, make my life count
☐ Fasting
☐ How to study the Bible
☐ Holy Spirit
☐ Books of the Bible
☐ Disciples
☐ Lifestyle assessment
☐ Temptation
☐ The church
☐ Guilt
☐ Ethics
☐ Worry/depression
☐ Abortion
☐ Temper
☐ Death and dying
☐ The tongue
☐ Euthanasia
☐ Satan
☐ Divorce
☐ Fruit of the Spirit
☐ Pacifism
☐ Doubt
☐ Stewardship
☐ Prayer
☐ Basics of the faith
☐ Worship
☐ Faith
☐ Sin

☐ Love
☐ Introduction to the New Testament
☐ Obedience
☐ Spiritual gifts
☐ Missions
☐ Rock music
☐ Other faiths
☐ Drugs
☐ Parent/child relationships
☐ Spiritual battles
☐ Dating
☐ The book of Revelation
☐ Authority, government
☐ Servanthood
☐ God's faithful promises
☐ The book of Genesis
☐ Prejudice
☐ Walking in the light
☐ Self-acceptance
☐ Who's who in the Bible
☐ Nuclear power
☐ Communication skills
☐ Relationships
☐ Family
☐ Materialism
☐ Life of Christ

☐ Peer pressure
☐ Christian apologetics
☐ Sermon on the Mount
☐ Perseverance
☐ Forgiveness
☐ Psalms
☐ Walk your talk
☐ Proverbs
☐ Gossip
☐ Prophecy
☐ Community
☐ Current events
☐ Careers
☐ The environment
☐ Evolution
☐ Balanced lifestyle
☐ Philosophy
☐ Discipline
☐ End times
☐ Christian vocations
☐ Body life
☐ Homosexuality
☐ Heaven
☐ Leisure time
☐ Drinking
☐ The body as God's temple
☐ Dealing with zits and bad breath
☐ Preparing for college

STUDENT SPONSOR SEARCH

Many students attribute their spiritual growth to significant people in their lives. Teaching students to find people who can build them up develops the ability to find those types of people in the future. The following idea is a practical way to put that plan to work.

A great way to get students involved in the process of recruiting volunteers is to survey the students and have them contact the potential volunteers. Take a survey asking questions like

1. Which of the adults in this church have had the most significant impact on your life?

2. Which of the adults do you most respect?

Compile the list, design a recruiting strategy, and let the students recruit the sponsors.

SPIRITUAL DISCOVERY

Another way to give students responsibility for their own growth is to teach using discovery instead of declaration. Truth that is discovered tends to have a stronger and more powerful impact on the life of a kid. The following are some effective ways to help students get involved in the process of spiritual discovery.

Workbooks are excellent tools to get students studying the Scriptures for themselves. Books like *Living Your Life . . . As God Intended, High School TalkSheets*, and *What'cha Gonna Do with What'cha Got?*[2] are outstanding for enabling students to learn for themselves. You can use these books and others like them individually and in groups. Give the students a few minutes to work on the workbook, then pull them together and let them share what they've learned.

Debates challenge students to begin to grapple with tough issues. We had a month-long debate with graduating seniors every year. We gave them the book *Know Why You Believe*,[3] and spent the month attacking their faith. They read the book, fought back, and for the first time began to get a grip on the reasons for their faith.

Giving students responsibility for their own spiritual growth is essential for their long-term spiritual health. "Jesus loves me, this I know, my youth pastor told me so," will not cut it on the college campus. The faith of a young teenager is usually dependent to a large degree upon the youth worker. Long-lasting spiritual growth is a process of weaning the student from dependence on us to dependence on the Lord. This is often tougher on the weaner than on the weanee. The bottom line in measuring effectiveness in youth ministry lies not in the number of students in your group, but in what your students do with their faith ten years after they graduate. Those students who own their own faith for the long haul will be those who have taken on responsibility for their own growth. That will take a little motivating, some delegating, and lots of encouraging.

Endnotes

1. Institute of American Church Growth (Pasadena, Calif., 1983), as quoted in Jim Burns, *The Youth Builder* (Eugene, Ore.: Harvest House, 1988), 116.

2. Jim Burns, *Living Your Life . . . As God Intended* (Eugene, Ore.: Harvest House, 1985); David Lynn, *High School TalkSheets* (Grand Rapids: YS/Zondervan, 1987); *What'cha Gonna Do with What'cha Got?* (Elgin, Ill.: David C. Cook, 1987).

3. Paul Little, *Know Why You Believe* (Wheaton, Ill.: Scripture Press/ Victor, 1987).

Resources for Leadership Development

Resources for Team Building

AN IMPORTANT PART OF THE leadership training process is the development of interpersonal skills. Today's students are growing up in what has been aptly described a "high tech-low touch" culture that includes few opportunities for developing the skills of communicating, negotiating, compromising, affirming, and listening. The following list gives program ideas for building teamwork and interpersonal skills into your leadership team.

BODY LIFE GAME

This game demonstrates the need for cooperation and unity within the body of Christ as presented in New Testament Scripture. Divide the entire group into five smaller groups that symbolize parts of the body. Each group should be named accordingly (for example, Eyes, Hands, Ears, Feet, and Mouth).

The object of the game is for the five groups, all members of the same body, to work together and perform their tasks before "Life" dies. To symbolize "Life," lock someone in a box and light a road flare nearby. When the flare goes out, "Life" will be considered dead. The only way "Life" can be saved is for the groups to complete the tasks that lead to the key that unlocks "Life" before the flare burns out (about thirty minutes).

Each of the five groups should be equal in size and labeled in some way (different color arm bands or signs). To complete the tasks, each group may work only as a normal body works; that is, Eyes can only see, and Ears can only hear. Therefore, everyone except the Eyes team members must be blindfolded.

When the game begins, the blindfolds go on, the flare is lit, and the group gets its first task. The instruction for that task is written down and presented to the Eyes, who whisper it to the Ears, who likewise whisper it to the Mouths, who then verbalize it to the rest of the body. Whenever the group must go anywhere, the Feet must carry the Eyes (the only ones who can see) and the remaining members of the body must follow in a single-file line, holding onto each other's waists. The Eyes in that case are allowed to speak, giving directions to the rest of the body.

The tasks may be relatively simple ones. Three or four good ones are enough. A few examples are listed here.

1. Crackers and juice should be fed to the Mouths by the Hands while being guided by the Eyes. The Feet will then carry the Ears to a designated place, followed by the rest of the body in a single-file line.

2. The Ears will be given a number (by the leader) between one and ten. The Ears must then hold up that many fingers for the Eyes to see, who then tell the Mouths, who shout it to the Hands and Feet. Everyone must then get in smaller groups of that number of people. The Eyes may help everyone get together. (This can be repeated.)

3. Splints and bandages can be provided for the Hands to use to splint one arm and one leg of each of the Feet, guided by the Eyes.

The above tasks are only samples. It is best to work out a few tasks that specifically fit your locality. The last task should lead to the envelope containing the key. The Hands must use the key to open the box, again guided by the Eyes and carried there by the Feet.

After-game discussion could include the following questions:

1. How did each part of the body function?

2. Did everyone do his or her part?

3. Why didn't some people get involved?

4. Relate this to Paul's analogy of the body (1 Corinthians 12:14-26).

Although this game seems simple, it must be thought through carefully by the leader before it's played. One youth group used three different bodies and three different keys representing "Faith," "Hope," and "Love." With a little creativity, the possibilities are endless.

CLIQUES AND LONERS

Here's an idea that gets kids talking about the effects of cliques on a youth group. Arrange the chairs in the room ahead of time to represent common groups of youths at a meeting.

1. A group of chairs in a circle all hooked together represents the group of teens who regularly attend the youth group.

2. A chair in the middle of the circle represents the person who

wants to be the center of attention.

3. A few chairs outside the group represent newcomers who don't feel part of the group in the circle.

4. A chair next to the door represents a person who has never come before.

5. A chair just outside the door represents someone who is afraid to come into the meeting.

6. A chair on top of the table represents a critical person who looks down on everyone in the group.

7. A broken chair that's different from all the others represents a person in the group who is a little different from the rest because of a handicap, a foreign accent, or some other distinction.

8. A small cluster of three to four chairs off from the large circle represents an exclusive clique.

You can probably think of some other ways to represent various groupings of your youths. There should be a chair for every student, with no chairs left over. Now tape a number to each chair. As each person arrives, give her or him a number at random corresponding to one of the chairs in the room. Tell the students they may not move the chairs and they must stay in their assigned seats during the entire meeting.

Be sensitive in your selection—choose certain kids who are part of established cliques as well as one or two of the loners to interview in front of the group. Ask the group to compare the experiences of the kids interviewed by discussing what the problems are and how they can be solved without destroying relationships or coercing friendships. Use the following questions to stimulate their thinking:

1. What is a clique?

2. What are the advantages or disadvantages of being in a clique?

3. What are the advantages or disadvantages of being a loner?

4. What would be the ideal situation in a youth group such as ours?

5. If Christ were in our group, where would he sit? Or would he be a loner?

6. What are some ways we can reach out to loners?

7. How can we develop positive groupings within our youth group?

COMMON GROUND

This activity "breaks the ice" by helping kids discover how much they have in common with each other. Divide the students into discussion groups of five to seven kids, and give each group a sheet listing a variety of categories (see list below). Each group must choose a secretary to record its preferences, and then come up with something that all the members like or all the members dislike in each category. Ask the kids to be honest instead of just going for the points.

For each item common to everyone in the group, give the group ten points. If, however, only five out of a group of seven have a particular thing in common, the group receives only five points. Set a time limit of ten minutes for this exercise.

CATEGORY	LIKE	DISLIKE
1. Food	____	____
2. Game	____	____
3. TV show	____	____
4. Gift received	____	____
5. School subject	____	____
6. Chore at home	____	____
7. Song	____	____
8. Hobby	____	____
9. Way to spend Saturday	____	____
10. Sport	____	____

During the next ten minutes, each group must list as many other shared experiences as it can. Anything is acceptable, as long as each person in the group has had that experience. For example:

1. I got a B on my last report card.

2. I've been sad over the death of a loved one.

3. I've been stood up by a friend.

4. I've been on a backpacking trip.

Give additional points for each shared experience. At the end of the time limit, the group totals up its points.

CONVERSATION HELPS

This is a list of questions designed to facilitate self-disclosure and discovery. Keep this list available—it may come in handy.

1. Share a time in your life when you were embarrassed.
2. If you received $5,000 as a gift, how would you spend it?
3. Of all the material possessions you have, what gives you the most pleasure?
4. If you could live anyplace in the world, where would it be?
5. If you could give the person on your right a fruit of the Spirit, which one would you give?
6. What part of a big parade would you like to be?
7. What do you think your friends say about you when you're not around?
8. How do you look when you get angry?
9. What is something that makes you feel sad?
10. Share a frightening moment.
11. In one sentence, what is life all about?
12. Describe heaven.
13. What is something that you feel God wants you to do?
14. Of what are you most afraid?
15. How would you describe peace?
16. What is the most childlike quality you've retained?
17. What do you like most about yourself?
18. What do you think about when you can't fall asleep?
19. Share a big letdown in your life.
20. What advice would you give a young bride?
21. What do you dislike most about yourself?
22. What would you like to invent to make life better?
23. If someone could give you anything in the world for your birthday, what would you like?
24. If you wrote a book today, what would the title be?
25. Share one of the happiest days of your life.
26. Share a personal spiritual experience.
27. What is something that really bugs you?
28. What does America mean to you?

29. Share a time when your feelings were hurt.

30. Share something that you fear.

31. Look at the person across from you and tell how you think you and he or she are related.

32. Say something about meditation.

33. When you are alone and no one can see you or hear you, what do you like to do?

34. What do you think makes a happy marriage?

35. What four things are most important in your life?

36. How would you define joy?

37. What is something that makes you angry?

38. If you could have been someone famous in history, who would it have been?

39. Name two famous people you'd like to have for parents.

40. If you were lost in the woods and it got dark, what would you do?

41. What makes a house a home?

42. Describe the perfect wife.

43. Describe the perfect husband.

44. What do you like to do in your spare time?

45. Tell about the neatest birthday present you ever received.

46. If you could change your age, what age would you rather be?

47. What really turns you on?

48. What is something you can do pretty well?

49. What kind of store would you like to own and operate?

50. If you were a doctor, what ailment would you like to cure?

51. What would you like to be remembered for after you die?

52. Describe the best teacher you ever had.

53. Thinking back, what can you identify as a turning point in your life?

54. Make a statement about courage.

55. If you could make a long distance phone call, who would you call?

56. If you became president of the United States, what two things would you do?

57. What bit of advice would you give a young man about to get married?

58. Complete the statement: "Words can't describe how I felt when . . ."

59. What talent do you wish you had?

60. What would you like to say to the person you see when you look in the mirror?

61. What is the most sentimental possession that you have?

62. Tell what makes a happy family.

63. If you had to move and could take only three things with you, what would you take?

64. Describe the ideal life.

65. What does freedom mean to you?

66. What lifetime dream are you still trying to make come true?

67. What TV or movie star would you like to invite to your birthday party?

68. What do you like to daydream about?

69. What kind of animal would you like to be, and where would you like to live?

70. If someone were to write a book about you, what do you think it would be called?

71. If you could receive a sixth sense, what would you want it to be?

72. If you believe in God, what do you base your belief on?

73. What things make your life complicated?

74. What kind of TV commercial would you like to make?

75. Share three things that you are thankful for.

76. If you were convinced that reincarnation was a fact, how would you like to come back?

77. What epitaph do you want on your tombstone?

78. What feelings do you have the most trouble expressing?

79. What is your favorite name for God?

80. If you could give any gift in the world, what would you give to the person on your right?

81. Say something about death.

82. If you were told you only have one week to live, how would you spend it?

83. What do you want to be doing in ten years?

84. What activity do you engage in that involves all of you: your heart, your mind, and your soul?

85. If you were asked to preach a sermon, what would the title be?

86. What character in the Bible do you relate to?

87. What went through your mind when the last person shared?

88. What do you feel is your purpose in life?

89. What is your favorite hymn or inspirational song?

90. What aspect of your life would you change if you decided to live Christ's teaching?

91. How can one know God's will for his or her life?

92. What spiritual goal are you reaching for?

93. What part of the Bible do you have difficulty understanding?

94. Share an experience of answered prayer.

95. How do *you* tune in to God?

ELECTRIC FENCE

This group game stresses teamwork and cooperation. It can be played just for fun, or you can debrief the experience with the group afterward to learn more about how the group works together to solve problems.

Tie a string or rope about five feet off the ground between two poles or objects. The object of the game is for the teams to get over the string (the "electric fence") without touching it. Divide the group into teams of ten or less, and have each group perform the task separately. The following rules apply: No one can go under the fence or around the fence, and no one is allowed to touch the poles or objects the string is tied to. In most cases, the group will have the most difficulty with the first person and the last person over the fence.

FIRST GUESS FAVORITE

For this mixer, print up copies of the game sheet on the next page (or make up your own) and give one to each person. First, each person chooses his or her own favorite in each category and then the kids circulate around the room trying to guess (on the first guess) the favorites of others in each category. If they successfully guess someone's favorite on the first try, then they put that person's initials to the right of that category on the guesser's sheet. The guesser with the most initials wins.

First Guess Favorite

Directions: First, put a check to the left of your own favorites in each category. Then circulate around the room and guess the favorites of others in the group. If you guess correctly on the first try, they initial to the right of the category on your sheet. No more than two initials from the same person.

1. Favorite music _____
   - ☐ Country and western
   - ☐ Classical
   - ☐ Rock and roll
   - ☐ Gospel

2. Favorite food _____
   - ☐ Mexican
   - ☐ American (meat and potatoes)
   - ☐ Chinese
   - ☐ Italian

3. Favorite car _____
   - ☐ Luxury
   - ☐ Sports
   - ☐ Economy
   - ☐ Truck

4. Favorite movies _____
   - ☐ Adventure
   - ☐ Comedy
   - ☐ Mystery
   - ☐ Science fiction

5. Favorite vacation _____
   - ☐ Beach
   - ☐ Mountains
   - ☐ World travel (plane, cruise)
   - ☐ Sightseeing America (by car)

6. Favorite sweet _____
   - ☐ Pie
   - ☐ Cake
   - ☐ Frozen (ice cream, yogurt)
   - ☐ Candy

7. Favorite animal _____
   - ☐ Dog
   - ☐ Cat
   - ☐ Bird
   - ☐ Exotic

8. Favorite TV show _____
   - ☐ News or news program
   - ☐ Comedy
   - ☐ Drama
   - ☐ Soap opera

9. Favorite reading material _____
   - ☐ Magazine
   - ☐ Fiction books
   - ☐ Nonfiction books
   - ☐ Newspapers

10. Favorite spectator sport _____
    - ☐ Football
    - ☐ Basketball
    - ☐ Baseball
    - ☐ Tennis or golf

11. Favorite color _____
    - ☐ Dark (black, brown, rust)
    - ☐ Light (white, tan)
    - ☐ Pastel (yellow, pink, baby blue)
    - ☐ Bright (red, blue)

12. Favorite season _____
    - ☐ Winter
    - ☐ Spring
    - ☐ Summer
    - ☐ Fall

13. Favorite time of day _____
    - ☐ Early morning
    - ☐ Afternoon
    - ☐ Evening
    - ☐ Late night

(**Source:** Wayne Rice, ed., *Ideas 43* [El Cajon, Calif.: Youth Specialties, 1987], 11.)

FOOT WASHING EXPERIENCE

Begin this meaningful experience in humility and service by reading John 13:1-18. After the reading, discuss questions like the following with the group:

1. Why did Jesus wash the disciples' feet?

2. Why was foot washing a custom in those days?

3. Who usually did the foot washing in those days?

4. How do you think the disciples felt when Jesus washed their feet?

5. How would you feel if Jesus washed your feet?

After the discussion, divide into groups of four or five. Give each group a water-filled dishpan and towels. Allow the students to take turns washing each other's feet. Encourage them to do it in the same spirit as Christ when he washed his disciples' feet.

Following this experience, ask the group to reflect on what happened: "How did this make you feel?" "Which was most difficult—washing or being washed?" "How can we symbolically wash each other's feet on a regular basis?"

FRAGILE FRIENDS

This exercise alerts kids to the fragility of other people and the importance of being gentle with each other. It can be used anytime but is especially appropriate for a camp or retreat.

Give each person a raw egg. Have each student punch a small hole in each end of his or her egg with a pin or nail and then blow on one end of the egg. The contents of the egg will be forced out the other end and an empty, unbroken eggshell will remain. The egg can be sealed up with a small amount of candle wax. The insides of the eggs can be served the next morning for breakfast.

Discuss with the kids how the delicate nature of the eggshells reflects the delicate nature of our relationships with each other. Then give the group several thin, colored marking pens that will write on the eggshells. Have the kids write the names of several kids in the group on the eggshells, being careful not to break the eggs.

Now each person must carry her or his egg all day, devising some means of protection and accepting responsibility for its condition. At the end of the day, collect the eggs, whole or smashed, and discuss the feelings of responsibility, the task of caring, and the problems of protecting something so fragile. Tie this in with how we treat each other personally and how we can avoid hurting each other.

THANKSGIVING EXCHANGE

Do this exercise, which teaches gratitude and affirmation, if your students know each other fairly well. Ask the teenagers to write his or her name across the top of a sheet of paper. Collect the papers and redistribute them so that each student has someone else's paper. Now have the kids write on the sheets what they would be thankful for if they were the person named on their page. They can list as many things as they want.

Your young people can exchange sheets several times so that several people have a chance to add to each list. The sheets should eventually be returned to the original owner. Give the kids time to read the comments on their sheets, and then allow those who want to share their list with the entire group to do so.

UNITY

This is an attempt to simulate unity and its meaning within your leadership team. To begin, read Ephesians 4:1-16 on "The Unity of the Body of Christ," and discuss what unity really means. What is Paul trying to say? How would we as a group illustrate Paul's description of unity?

Bring out enough Tinker Toys so that every member of the group has plenty to work with. There must be plenty of space for people to work. The best place is in a large carpeted room where everyone can sit on the floor. If this is not possible, then put groups of four people each at large tables. Once seated, explain that each person has five minutes of silence to think about himself or herself—who am I, what do I believe in, what do I want to be, and so on.

At the end of this period, allow five more minutes of silence for the students to build out of Tinker Toys who they think they are. At the end of this five-minute period, have each individual, again in silence, find a partner and for ten minutes (five minutes apiece) attempt to put the two objects together. The partners can only nod their heads "yes" or "no" as an indicator to the other. At the end of this ten-minute period, allow another ten minutes for the students to explain verbally what their objects stand for and why they would or would not allow certain parts of their objects to be connected with their partners'.

At the end of this ten-minute period, the two people should seek out two others and, in silence, attempt to put their objects together within ten minutes. At the end of this silent period, allow the four members to explain their objects to the others and why they would or would not connect their objects at certain parts. Now let the four partners find four more people and repeat the process until all the objects are united into one object and all players have had an opportunity to explain what their objects stand for. Now read Ephesians 4:1-16 once more and everyone ought to be able to see unity in diversity as Paul has explained it.

UPPERS AND DOWNERS

For an excellent exercise in community building, have the kids in your group fill out a chart similar to the one on the next page.

Give the kids the following directions for filling out the chart: Ask them to think of a time when someone said something to them that was really a "downer"—something that made them feel bad. This could be a put-down, an angry comment, anything. Then have them think of a time when someone said an "upper" to them—something that made them feel good. If they can think of several entries for the first two columns, encourage them to write them in.

Next, have the kids do the same thing in the third and fourth columns, only this time they should think of times when they said an "upper" or a "downer" to someone else.

OTHERS		ME	
Upper	Downer	Upper	Downer

If your students are typical, they'll be able to think of many more "downers" than "uppers." Discuss how easy it is to discourage or to put down others, how damaging our tongue can be, and how the damage takes a long time to repair.

Follow up with a look at Hebrews 10:23-25, which deals with encouragement, and then discuss practical ways to live out this Scripture.

You can also help kids recognize whether the things they say to each other are "uppers" or "downers." Some may even take the hint and learn to be more careful about what they say. If you are on a weekend retreat, challenge them to confront each other during the retreat when they hear someone giving someone else a "downer." This can cut down on the negativism that often ruins youth group meetings and activities.

WORKERS IN THE CHURCH

This small group activity is good for helping people build positive relationships with each other. It also helps people to see how different they all are, yet how important they are to the whole body of Christ. Give each person a list similar to the one below and have him or her write in the names of the people in the group who fit each job. Discussion may follow with each person explaining the choices made.

- *The Church Carpenter:* Someone who knows how to build solid, secure, and long-lasting relationships with others.
- *The Church Electrician:* Someone who adds that extra "spark" to the life of the church.
- *The Church Engineer:* Someone with the ability to plan things and to make sure that they are done right.
- *The Church Baker:* Someone who adds just the right amount of yeast to every occasion so that it rises successfully.
- *The Church Security Guard:* Someone who watches out for the welfare of the church and those in it. A person concerned about the well-being of others.
- *The Church Seamstress:* Someone who has the ability to sew the little tears back together. A person who is always able to patch things up.
- *The Church Custodian:* Someone who always seems willing to do the dirty jobs that no one else wants to do. A person who always makes things look a little better than they were.
- *The Church Tour Guide:* Someone who seems to have the ability to show others the right way to go.
- *The Church Attorney:* Someone who stands up on behalf of others and pleads their causes. A person who is concerned with justice and equity.
- *The Church Publicity Agent:* Someone so excited about the Christian life that he or she can't keep quiet about it.
- *Other:* (Write your own.)

Resources for Training Camps and Retreats

BECAUSE OF THE CONCENTRATED AMOUNT of time you spend with students at a retreat, you may be able to accomplish more than you would in months of meetings. A good leadership retreat will enable you to build unity, begin training, and generate motivation all in the same weekend. Four types of retreats are especially effective in the development of leadership ability.

LEADERSHIP DEVELOPMENT RETREAT

Used mainly at the start of the year (or whenever your first leadership team begins), this is usually the best type of retreat for bringing together the new leadership team. Some essentials should be taken into consideration.

Retreat Site—It will usually be smaller and more informal due to the limited size of the group. We have used homes of church members in resort areas with great success.

Retreat Goals—Beginning the leadership training process will facilitate opportunity to accomplish a number of objectives.

a. To create unity (use a lot of relational games—see Chapter Seven for ideas).

b. To transfer ownership and responsibility into the hands of the student leaders. Much of the time should be used for planning and giving direction for the whole group. It may be helpful to use the Yearly Planning Survey, the Content Survey, and the Event Planning Sheet at this stage. Remember, the greater the involvement, the greater the sense of ownership.

c. To enable the ministry teams to set goals and to make plans for their areas of responsibility. A great way to increase involvement and creativity is to list all of the leadership areas and allow the whole group to brainstorm ten great ideas for each area. The groups then take that input and use that as they set goals and make plans for the year.

d. To enable spiritual growth and development. These are your committed leaders, and these folks may be ready for mature spiritual growth material. Use a variety of methods to communicate, but make sure this is discipling, growth-oriented material.

e. To train and develop leadership ability. The following topics can be covered at the retreat:
  • The importance of youth ministry.
  • How to lead a Bible study.
  • How to prepare and give a youth talk.
  • How to teach junior high Sunday school and live to tell about it.
  • How to discover and develop your spiritual gifts.
  • How to set goals.
  • How to get organized.
  • How to manage your time.
  • How to share Christ on your campus.
  • How to study the Bible for yourself.
  • How to lead small groups.
  • How to build friendships.
  • How to become a disciple.
  • How to be a friend to a friend in crisis.

There are many ways to cover these topics: speakers, experts from your congregation, videos, and workbooks. You may want to assign topics to some of the teenagers, give them resource materials, and have them come prepared to teach each other.

YOUTH MINISTRY TRAINING EXPERIENCES

Many churches and organizations sponsor youth ministry training events in your area. Take your student leaders to conventions, workshops, seminars, and clinics. Occasionally (with a great deal of planning), we have taken students out of school to attend the Youth Specialties National Resource Seminar, a one-day training workshop held in seventy cities around the country. The kids spend the day with hundreds of youth workers, being treated like adults. Many students never recover from the experience.

STRESS CAMPING

These types of camps vary from river rafting to rock climbing and put kids in stressful situations. A skillful leader can use these types of experiences to develop leadership and character.

MISSIONS AND SERVICE CAMPS

Perhaps no other experience is as effective for developing commitment and leadership as a cross-cultural mission trip. The trip will be especially beneficial if the students are involved in the project planning, training, and leading. An outstanding resource for getting this type of retreat started is *The Complete Student Missions Handbook*, by Ridge Burns with Noel Becchetti (Grand Rapids: YS/Zondervan, 1990).

Two good additional resources that may provide help in this area are Chap Clark's *The Youth Specialties Handbook for Great Camps and Retreats* (Grand Rapids: YS/Zondervan, 1990); and "The Complete Retreat Outline," *Group* (May 1983) P.O. Box 481, Loveland, CO 80539, which offers a helpful checklist for planning retreats.

Content Ideas
for Training Meetings

THE FOLLOWING IS A LIST of ideas and resources that can be used in training meetings with student leaders. These ideas fit with the leadership planning worksheet in Chapter Eight.

Twelve Commandments that Ensure Failure of a Youth Group

The following "commandments" are twelve ways to make sure a youth group goes down the drain. A helpful list of "no-no's" for anyone involved in group leadership, this will make for an excellent training session.

1. **Wipe Out Incentive.** Tell the group members that someone tried their ideas six years ago. It didn't work then, and it won't work now!

2. **Depend on Only a Few Teens.** Use a few favorites for every activity and privilege. Don't try to develop responsibility in others.

3. **Don't Encourage or Affirm.** Take the kids and their efforts for granted.

4. **Focus on the Weaknesses of Others.** Never bother to pray that your students will be strengthened. Just scold them for their faults.

5. **Expect Everyone to Conform to Your Way of Thinking.** This covers everything! Whatever might happen, you are always right!

6. **Don't Try to Develop Group Spirit and Morale.** Why waste precious time developing traits they should have developed long ago?

7. **Don't Spend Time Building Friendships.** Tell the kids you are too busy to listen to their problems; besides, you have enough problems of your own.

8. **Betray Confidences.** As an illustration, use a confidence given to you by one of your friends in your youth meeting.

9. **Set Up a Spy System.** Ask your pets to report any "questionable" things going on among their friends. It will foster doubt and mistrust, to say nothing of disunity.

10. **Blame Your Failure as a Leader on the Others in the Group.** We will let you define this point yourself . . . no one knows better than you who is really to blame.

11. **Make Christianity a Religion of Don'ts.** Be sure to capitalize on all of the "no-no's" of Christianity. That is much easier than teaching that the Christian life is a healthy, disciplined freedom, offering opportunity for our own self-expression and the taking on of responsibilities.

12. **Be a Grouch.** No one likes anyone better than an all-around grouch. It does wonders for the morale and spirit of the entire group!

BODY BUILDING

Group Leader: You will lead your group through this activity. Introduce this activity by saying something like, "We have already talked about and seen how all parts of the body work together or are supposed to work together. Our unity as the body of Christ—our fellowship—means that we have a special relationship to one another. In Ephesians 4:22-32, Paul explains some aspects of the daily practice of that kind of fellowship."

Divide your group in half. Ask one person from each half to read the passage aloud. Then have each of the halves compose a skit demonstrating the ways we often break down the sort of fellowship that Paul is talking about in these verses.

For example: In verses 26 and 27, Paul writes, "In your anger do not sin: Do not let the sun go down while you are still angry, and do not give the devil a foothold." These verses seem to be saying that anger itself is not so bad—we all get angry occasionally—but it must be dealt with quickly so that it does not grow into bitterness and hatred.

One of your groups might base its skit on these verses by portraying someone whose feelings have been hurt by another and how, instead of dealing with that hurt immediately, he or she stews for a few days, getting angrier. The next time they meet, the offender becomes the victim of this person's growing anger and instead of the two making peace, the situation grows worse.

Have the two groups present their skits to the whole group. After each skit, as you have time, discuss the following questions:

1. Where did the fellowship break down in the situation portrayed? Which of the muscles of Ephesians 4:2 did not get flexed?

2. What specific verse of Ephesians 4:22-32 is related to this situation? How would the situation have changed if the people involved had applied this verse?

Diagnosis: To close this session, ask your students to diagnose the condition of their youth group "body." Ask each group member to think for a minute about these questions.

Is your "body" healthy?

Is your group suffering from paralysis?

How about heart trouble?

Is it suffering from lack of coordination?

From poor vision?

From lack of hearing?

Have each member make his or her own diagnosis.

Prescription: Have each person refer to what was observed in Ephesians 4:1-5 and 22-32 to find a prescription for whatever problems have been observed. For example, one person might say, "Our group has a sore throat. We seem to gossip a lot and cut each other down. We need a healthy dose of Ephesians 4:29."

Give each student a chance to share his or her personal diagnosis and prescription.

COST OF DISCIPLESHIP

The following are four significant New Testament Scriptures dealing with discipleship and what it means. The questions under each passage are excellent discussion starters to help your group focus on the main issue of each passage. This exercise is most effective if done with small groups of five to ten kids.

Pass out a copy of the questions below and have the young people circle what they consider to be the best answer for each question. There is also a space to write an answer if they feel none of the others is sufficient.

Cost of Discipleship

Read Luke 9:23-25.

1. To me "taking up my cross daily" means
   a. Doing things I hate to do.
   b. Facing death.
   c. Being teased because I am a Christian.
   d. Accepting anything that God desires of me as part of his plan for my life.
   e. None of the above.

   f. _____

2. "Denying self" means denying anything that would prevent complete commitment to Christ. For me this has meant
   a. Nothing, as I haven't made this type of commitment yet.
   b. Nothing, as I don't understand how to do this.
   c. Attempting to quit being lazy in my job at home, school, work, or church.
   d. Not trying so hard, and letting Christ take over.
   e. Giving up my favorite TV show to come to youth group meetings.

   f. _____

Read John 17:13-24.

1. Being "one" here means
   a. Doing things together.
   b. Never disagreeing and always accepting the other's viewpoint.
   c. Learning to love, to share, and to work closely with each other.

   d. _____

2. This "oneness" can be achieved by
   a. Denying ourselves and sharing our gut feelings with each other.
   b. No longer disagreeing with others.
   c. Getting to know others in the group better.
   d. It's too difficult, so I won't try.

   e. _____

Read 1 John 3:23, 24; John 13:34, 35.

1. This type of love means
   a. Action—sharing myself with others.
   b. Attitude—finding the good in other people.
   c. Loving others enough to help them with their problems.
   d. All of the above.

   e. _____

2. A "personal relationship with God" to me means
   a. Asking Christ to forgive me.
   b. Having visions of God talking to me.
   c. It won't really happen until I get to heaven.
   d. Accepting Christ as my best friend.

   e. _____

Read 1 Corinthians 15:49; 1 John 3:2.

1. Becoming like Christ means
   a. Sinning less and less.
   b. Learning to love as Christ loved.
   c. Learning to minister for Christ.
   d. Growing in knowledge of God and the Bible.

   e. _____

Gift Guessing

This game helps kids focus on the discovery and use of spiritual gifts. Prepare ahead of time adhesive labels listing various gifts or qualities like *teacher*, *counselor*, *leader*, *helper*, and *listener*. When each student arrives, place a label on his or her back without revealing what it says. The kids then mingle around the room and try to guess their gifts. Each person asks someone else, "What is my gift?" The person who is asked may not talk, but must communicate only by pantomime or charades.

Once a person has guessed her or his gift, the sticker may be worn on the front like a name tag and the student continues to help others guess. After everyone has guessed the gifts, allow the kids to exchange their gifts with others or get new name tags and write any gift on it that they feel is more apt to be theirs.

Follow up with discussion and affirmation of each other's gifts and abilities.

The Lifesaving Station

This short parable is great for discussion or as a simple thought-provoker on the subjects of the church and the world. It may be read aloud (or printed and passed out to your group), followed by a discussion using the questions that are provided. The story was written by Theodore Wedel of Washington, D.C. (**Source:** Wayne Rice, ed., *Ideas 5 8* [El Cajon, Calif.: Youth Specialties, 1979, 1984], 78.)

On a dangerous seacoast where shipwrecks often occurred, there was once a crude little lifesaving station. The building was just a hut, and there was only one boat, but the few devoted members kept a constant watch over the sea. With no thought for themselves, they went out day and night, tirelessly searching for the lost. Some of those who were saved, and various others in the surrounding area, wanted to become associated with the station and give of their time, money, and effort for the support of its work. New boats were bought and new crews trained. The little lifesaving station grew.

Some of the members of the lifesaving station were unhappy that the building was so crude and poorly equipped. They felt that a more comfortable place should be provided as a first refuge for those saved from the sea. They replaced the emergency cots with beds and put better furniture in the enlarged building. Now the lifesaving station became a popular gathering place for its members, and they decorated it beautifully and furnished it exquisitely, because they used it as a sort of club. Fewer members were now interested in going to sea on lifesaving missions, so they hired lifeboat crews to do this work. The lifesaving motif still prevailed in this club's decoration, and there was a liturgical lifeboat in the room where the club initiations were held. About this time, a large ship was wrecked off the coast, and the hired crews brought in boatloads of cold, wet, and half-drowned people. They were dirty and sick; some of them had black skin and some had yellow skin. The beautiful new club was in chaos. So the property committee immediately had a shower house built outside the club where victims of shipwreck could be cleaned up before coming inside.

At the next meeting, there was a split in the club membership. Most of the members wanted to stop the club's lifesaving activities because they were unpleasant and a hindrance to the normal social life of the club. Some members insisted upon lifesaving as their primary purpose and pointed out that they were still called a lifesaving station. But they were finally voted down and told that if they wanted to save lives of all the various kinds of people who were shipwrecked in those waters, they could begin their own lifesaving station down the coast. They did.

As the years went by, the new station experienced the same changes that had occurred in the old. It evolved into a club, and yet another lifesaving station was founded. History continued to repeat itself, and if you visit that seacoast today, you will find a number of exclusive clubs along that shore. Shipwrecks are frequent in those waters, but most of the people drown.

Questions for Discussion

1. When was the lifesaving station most effective?

2. Where did the lifesaving station go wrong?

3. How is the church like a lifesaving station? What is the purpose of the church?

4. Is growth always good or desirable?

5. Is growth inevitable if needs are being met?

6. If you don't like the church as it is now, what alternatives do you have?

7. What should the church do with all of its money?

8. How can the problems that the lifesaving station experienced be avoided in the church? What should the lifesaving station have done?

9. Is the church necessary for being a Christian?

10. What are your church's good points? Bad points?

11. If you could write a moral for the lifesaving station story, what would it be?

THE PULPIT COMMITTEE

Have your group learn about the apostle Paul and discuss qualifications for spiritual leadership by using this simple strategy.

Divide the group into a number of small "pulpit committees" each with the task of securing a new minister for your congregation. Have the group compile a list of characteristics that they feel the candidates should have, then give them several "applications." Be sure to include the following letter among them:

Gentlemen:

Understanding your pulpit is vacant, I should like to apply for the position. I have many qualifications. I have met with much success as a preacher and also as a writer. Some say I'm a good organizer. I've been a leader most places I've been. Although I'm older than fifty, I have never preached in one place for more than three years. In some places, I have left town after my work has caused riots and disturbances. I must admit I have been in jail three or four times, but not because of any real wrongdoing. My health is not too good, though I still get a great deal done. The churches I have preached in have been small, though located in several large cities. I've not gotten along well with religious leaders in towns where I've preached. In fact, some have threatened me and even attacked me physically. Also, I am not too good at keeping records; I have been known to forget whom I have baptized. However, if you can use me, I shall do my best for you.

Go over the findings and reveal to the group that the letter above describes the apostle Paul. Then go on to study what true spiritual leadership requires.

SIMULATED PLANNING MEETING

This idea works best with a new youth group or a new group of officers and it can very effectively demonstrate how group dynamics work. Assign different officers or members of the group the characters listed below. Give them typewritten sheets with instructions and allow them a few minutes to think through how they are going to act. No one is to know what the others' descriptions say, and you must make it very clear that it will be more effective if the participants do not attempt to overact. This is not a skit. The rest of the group can simply watch and observe while the cast of characters "plans" an activity, program, or social event.

- *The Enthusiastic Leader:* You are pro-youth group and are really excited about getting the group going. You see a lot of potential in the group and sincerely want it to go well. You are vocal, and you take the lead. You try to get everyone to cooperate, and discourage negative thinking. You maintain order and keep things from getting off track or too boring. You are a person who tries not to reject anyone. Rather than dominating the meeting with your ideas, you try to get everyone working together, focusing on one goal.

- *The Follower:* You are supportive of anything positive. You are really excited about the youth group and want to see it go. Try to help and cooperate in any way you can. You have a lot to contribute.

- *The Negative Influence:* You are not too sure the youth group is such a great idea. You ask questions because you are skeptical of anything working out with the kids you know. Don't say anything positive—point out the problems that need to be considered. Try to postpone decision making and delay coming to conclusions or action. Note: Don't be too obvious. Just say enough to be effective.

- *The Pathetic Apathetic:* You are not interested in anything. You are indifferent—neither positive nor negative. Be bored and say so in your own words; be sarcastic. Treat the entire activity as a waste of time. Note: Be careful and don't overdo it!

- *The Reactor:* React to whatever happens in the group. If you think someone is being too negative, then confront that person and find out why. If someone is messing around and it bothers you or the group, confront him or her. If you notice that someone is bored or uninterested, then try to get the individual's attention and generate some interest. If that doesn't work, ask what the problem is. You see your role as a peacekeeper and an in-between person who tries to bring out the best in each person in the group.

- *The Goof-off:* Do what comes naturally. Make jokes and don't take anything seriously. Try to have lots of fun. Be mildly disruptive. Note: Do not overdo it; do just enough to have a good time without arousing hostility.

After a fair amount of time, fifteen to twenty minutes, end the "planning meeting" and discuss what happened. Did the group accomplish anything? Why or why not? What contributed to the planning meeting? What hindered the planning meeting? Could you identify different roles? What makes a good planning group?

SMALL GROUP LEADERSHIP

"How do I care?" This is a content exercise designed to motivate involvement and caring. There are three steps in learning how to care. Help your kids learn them.

Step One: Identify who needs care. The first task in learning how to care for others is to identify those around us who need the care. We get overwhelmed when told our job is to "love the whole world." If we open our eyes, we can put a name to the face or group near us who needs our care. Knowing "his" name and what "she's" like or where "they" live helps us get excited about caring.

Activity: Denny Rydberg, "The Outsiders," from *Building Community in Youth Groups* (Loveland, Colo.: Group Books, 1985), 134-35.

1. Pick one or two people to be the "outsiders."

2. Have the remaining members of the group stand in a circle close together. The people forming the circle are supposed to try to keep the "outsiders" from getting inside the circle.

3. Instruct the "outsiders" to try to get inside the circle. This is a physical activity, so be careful: Make sure the activity doesn't get out of hand. If one person struggles, but can't get inside, give someone else a try.

Discussion:

1. How did you react to being an "outsider"?

2. How did it feel to try keeping the "outsiders" from gaining entry into the group?

3. Have someone read Matthew 25:31-46.
   a. Describe the sheep and then the goats. What are the differences between them?
   b. Why did the sheep inherit the kingdom?
   c. According to this story, who are the "outsiders"?

4. Who are the "outsiders" in your world today? Stretch your thinking a bit. Identify who the "outsiders" are in your youth group, at school, in your community, in our country, and in the world. Be specific—use names, don't just say "the poor." Identify who the poor people are and where they live. Develop a list of all the "outsiders" your group can think of.

Step Two: Start small. The challenge of caring for all the people on your list is monumental, if not impossible. The temptation is to get overwhelmed, get frustrated, and give up. Here is a helpful phrase worth remembering: Something is better than nothing.

Rather than trying to care for the world all at once, start small, pick one person or group, and begin to help them. Remember, doing one thing is better than doing nothing.

Starting small can mean starting with those who are closest to us. Caring for a family member or a neighbor across the street today can help us learn how to love a neighbor across the ocean tomorrow.

Activity:

1. Select from your list of "outsiders" one group or person who needs your tangible help before this week is over. Group or person(s) we want to help:

   _____

2. Select from your list of "outsiders" one group or person in your hometown needing your tangible help before the year is over. Group or person(s) we want to serve:

   _____

Step Three: Give rather than take. Sometimes we make caring for other people too hard. Really, it's quite simple. Caring means giving something we have to someone else. Jesus says it can even be a cup of water given, in his name, to someone who is thirsty.

Activity:

1. Go back to Matthew 25:31-46.
   a. What character quality separated the sheep from the goats?

b. What simple things did the sheep do to receive God's blessing?

2. Come up with your own definition of the verb *to care*.

_____

_____

_____

3. Brainstorm as a group one specific, tangible gift you can give, in Jesus' name, to the group or person(s) that you selected to help before the week is out. What will you do? When will you do it? Be creative!

What _____

When _____

4. What is one specific, tangible gift you can give, in Jesus' name, to the group or person(s) in your community that you selected to help before the year is out? What will you do? When will you do it? Be creative!

What _____

When _____

Conclude with a prayer for each other that God will give you strength and love as you serve Christ by serving others.

Unwanted Guest

Most youth groups don't easily make new people feel welcome. Assimilating strangers can be made easier, however, with this tried-and-tested project. Arrange for a kid from another youth group (far enough away so as not to be recognized) to come and spend a Sunday in your church. No one in your group should know about the setup—the students will think the teen is simply a typical visitor. Your guest should be dressed normally but not stylishly, should be friendly but quiet, and should speak only when spoken to. (This may take some acting.) He or she should come to Sunday school, church, maybe a softball game that afternoon (that you'll set up in advance), and a get-together after church that night.

That evening let your group know that the visitor was a "plant." Introduce him or her to the group and let the visitor report to your kids about the reception and treatment that was received. If you want to get really heavy, have your guest share with the group how some kids went out of their way to either accept or ignore him or her. Some kids will

151

want to crawl under the tables, and others will feel as if they have finally done something right.

Conclude with a discussion of the obstacles and fears that might keep youth group members from welcoming an outsider. Or, have the group complete this sentence: "The main reason I find it hard to welcome someone from outside our group is. . . ." Then talk about what the group or individuals can do to overcome these obstacles.

WAYS TO SERVE GOD

To help your youths think about how they can put their faith into action, pass out the following list of ten statements and have each person circle "T" for true and "F" for false next to each one. Then have a discussion based on their answers.

Ways to Serve God

T F 1. The only way to serve God is to be a pastor.

T F 2. You cannot serve God at school.

T F 3. If you're being paid for a job, it can't be service to God.

T F 4. Only certain people can serve God.

T F 5. We should serve God only on Sundays.

T F 6. Feeding ducks is serving God.

T F 7. Serving God may require sacrifice.

T F 8. Men serve God better than women.

T F 9. Driving the church van is serving God.

T F 10. Getting good grades has nothing to do with serving God.

(**Source:** Wayne Rice, ed., *Ideas 41* [El Cajon, Calif: Youth Specialties, 1986], 34.)

To explore the subject in more depth, break into small groups and assign each group one of these five topics to brainstorm: Ways to serve God in

1. our personal lives

2. our families

3. our church

4. our community

5. the world

Then let a spokesperson for each group report its ideas back to the entire group. By the end of the program, you'll have a long list of ways the youths can serve God. Type up the list and give it out at the next meeting.

WHAT A CHARACTER!

Teenagers seldom attract attention for having positive character qualities. This exercise helps students study biblical principles regarding character and affirm each other in the process. Have each student give an example of each of the following traits and then list a person in the group that he or she feels exhibits this trait.

Essential Qualities

EXAMPLE   GROUP MEMBER

1 Corinthians 13:4-8
- Patient
- Kind
- Not irritable
- Not envious
- Not jealous
- Not arrogant
- Not rude
- Not selfish
- Doesn't brag
- Doesn't demand own way

1 Timothy 3:2-13
- Thoughtful
- Orderly
- Full of good deeds
- Enjoys having guests in home
- Obedient to parents
- Hardworking
- Earnest follower of Christ
- Not greedy for money
- Well thought of by people outside the church
- Good Bible teacher

Titus 1:7-9
- Not self-willed
- Not quick-tempered
- Not addicted to wine
- Knows Bible
- Hospitable
- Sensible
- Just
- Self-controlled

Galatians 5:22-23
- Love, joy, peace
- Patience
- Kindness
- Goodness, gentleness
- Faithfulness
- Self-control

WHAT ARE MY GIFTS?

The atmosphere for this activity is crucial—the group needs to be relaxed, unhurried, and comfortable with each other. Photocopy the list of character traits below (add others if you want to) and distribute it to your group members. Ask them to read the list and then check three gifts they believe are their strongest traits. Next, ask them to write an "R" beside those character qualities that they think best apply to the person sitting on their immediate right. Finally, have them write an "L" next to those traits that best apply to those on their left.

Now, one at a time, have the two students on either side of one member read their lists that presumably describe that member. Then let the member read her or his own self-description. Ask the member to describe how she or he felt about the others' descriptions. Open the discussion up to the entire group before moving on to the next person.

This may take some time so, if you have a large group, do a few people each meeting for several weeks.

List of Traits

1. Compassion
2. Ability to listen
3. Trustworthiness
4. Loyalty
5. Sympathy
6. Caring
7. Cheerfulness
8. Ability to cheer others up
9. Helpfulness
10. Ability to make someone who's hurting feel better
11. Ability to mediate between two people or groups
12. Encouragement
13. Teaching
14. Humor
15. Ability to get things done
16. Vision for what the future can be
17. Hospitality—makes people feel comfortable
18. Perseverance/tenacity—ability to hang in there
19. Directness—doesn't play games
20. Independence—is not influenced by fads or trends
21. Nurturing—ability to help people grow
22. Organization
23. Creativity
24. Acceptance—ability to accept others
25. Diplomacy—ability to see two sides of an issue
26. Spirituality
27. Humility
28. Hopefulness
29. Optimism
30. Charity—ability to give everything freely
31. Faithfulness
32. Forgiveness
33. Sensitivity
34. Perception—ability to see beyond the superficial level

35. Other _____

36. Other _____

37. Other _____

38. Other _____

Bibliography: Books and Resources for Leadership Training and Development

Compiled by Paul Borthwick

Adams, Arthur M. *Effective Leadership in Today's Church*. Philadelphia: Westminster, 1978. Discusses issues such as running committee meetings, effective delegation, and authority in ministry.

Anderson, James D., and Ezra Earl Jones. *The Ministry of the Laity*. New York: Harper and Row, 1985. Defines ways to help laypeople see the ministry as their own rather than as the work of the professional.

Any Old Time Series. Wheaton, Ill.: Victor. Eight books of creative meeting ideas (with openers, Bible studies, discussions, panels, quizzes, polls, case studies, games, dramas, and retreats) on topics like crisis, life decisions, friends, outreach, the church, and Bible study.

Armerding, Hudson T. *Leadership*. Wheaton, Ill.: Tyndale House, 1978. A good tool for evaluating whether or not you're living up to the ideals and challenges of leading others.

Benson, Warren S., and Mark H. Senter, III. *The Complete Book of Youth Ministry*. Chicago: Moody Press, 1987. A compendium of articles from youth ministry leaders on the basic realms of youth work in which every leader must grow.

Blandford, Brian. *Winners and Losers*. Ventura, Calif.: Regal Books, 1985. A Bible study tool that looks at positive and negative examples of biblical characters. Useful as a motivator with Christian students.

Bonhoeffer, Dietrich. *The Cost of Discipleship*. New York: Macmillan, 1967. An enduring call to lead others by following the example of true discipleship lived out by "costly grace."

Borthwick, Paul. *How to Plan, Develop, and Lead a Youth Missionary Team*. Lexington, Mass.: Grace Chapel, 1980. A programmatic resource for designing missions projects for youth groups.

Bridges, Jerry. *The Pursuit of Holiness*. Colorado Springs: NavPress, 1983. Mandatory reading for every teacher who believes that living a holy life is more important than teaching it.

Bruce, A. B. *The Training of the Twelve*. Grand Rapids: Kregel, 1979. The classic, exhaustive study of the teaching and training methods Jesus used with his disciples.

Burns, Jim, and Doug Fields. *Congratulations! You Are Gifted!* Eugene, Ore.: Harvest House, 1986.

Burns, Ridge, with Noel Becchetti. *The Complete Student Missions Handbook*. Grand Rapids: YS/Zondervan, 1990.

Campbell, David. *If I'm in Charge Here, Why Is Everybody Laughing?* Niles, Ill.: Argus Communications, 1980. Identifies problems related to leadership in the church and suggests ways to negotiate and overcome opposition with diplomacy.

Campolo, Anthony. *You Can Make a Difference*. Waco, Tex.: Word, 1984. An excellent tool for motivating teenagers by giving them a more positive perspective on their potential.

Christie, Les. *How to Recruit and Train Volunteer Youth Workers*. Grand Rapids: YS/Zondervan, 1991. How to build a team of volunteers, including discussions of recruitment, training, ego, and envy in team ministry. (Previously published as *Unsung Heroes*.)

Clinton, Robert. *The Making of a Leader*. Colorado Springs: NavPress, 1988. Somewhat technical, yet still very helpful in identifying your own educational "phase" in growth.

Conklin, Robert. *How to Get People to Do Things*. Chicago: Contemporary, 1979. A motivational guide for leaders, this book contains with many insights on the power of affirmation and the recognition of others.

Coopersmith, Stanley. *The Antecedents of Self-Esteem*. Palo Alto, Calif.: Consulting Psychology Press, 1967; rept. 1981.

Covey, Steven R. *The Seven Habits of Highly Effective People*. New York: Simon and Schuster, 1989. A consultant to corporate executives reveals the habits most commonly found in leaders. A challenging book regarding self learning.

DePree, Max. *Leadership Is an Art*. New York: Doubleday, 1989. A rambling-style volume from a corporate executive on how to help people learn to work together. Excellent insights transferable to training volunteers and building team morale.

Discipleship Journal. Colorado Springs: The Navigators. A six-year-old bimonthly dedicated to personal learning, discipleship, and spiritual growth.

Dobson, James. *Preparing for Adolescence*. New York: Bantam Books, 1980. An excellent teaching guide for youths and parents. Other Dobson books include *Dare to Discipline* (Wheaton, Ill.: Tyndale House, 1970); *Hide or Seek* (Old Tappan, N.J.: Revell, 1974); *The Strong-Willed Child* (Wheaton, Ill.: Tyndale House, 1978); and *Emotions—Can You Trust Them?* (Ventura, Calif.: Regal, 1981).

Doering, Jeanne. *The Power of Encouragement*. Chicago: Moody Press, 1982. Good instructions on positive relationship building through encouragement. Necessary reading for a church staff team.

Drucker, Peter. *Management*. New York: Harper and Row, 1973. An administrative text that contains principles that can be useful in planning and carrying out a budget.

Elkind, David. *All Grown Up and No Place To Go*. Reading, Mass.: Addison-Wesley, 1984. Insightful book on the problems caused when teenagers are forced to grow up too fast.

Gellerman, Saul W. *Management by Motivation*. New York: American Management Association, 1968. A prize-winning book on motivation and productivity, with concepts that are transferable for use with volunteers.

Hendricks, Howard G. *Teaching to Change Lives*. Portland, Ore.: Multnomah Press, 1987. Seven well-illustrated concepts to make teaching more effective in the lives of students.

Hyde, Douglas. *Dedication and Leadership*. Notre Dame, Ind.: University of Notre Dame, 1966. A former Communist illustrates the training techniques of radical causes and applies them to the principles of Christian discipleship.

Johnson, Douglas W. *The Care and Feeding of Volunteers.* Nashville: Abingdon, 1978. Practical advice on recruiting, training, and motivating leadership teams.

Kesler, Jay, ed. *Parents and Teenagers.* Wheaton, Ill.: Victor, 1984. Contributions by over fifty Christian leaders on a host of family-related subjects. Articles are pithy and application-oriented.

LePeau, Andrew T. *Paths of Leadership.* Downers Grove, Ill.: InterVarsity Press, 1983. Useful in evaluating leadership styles.

Leypoldt, Martha M. *Learning is Change.* Valley Forge, Pa.: Judson Press, 1971. Identifies the crucial need for practical change as a result of learning.

Lynn, David, and Mike Yaconelli. *Tension Getters* (Volumes One and Two). Grand Rapids: YS/Zondervan, 1981, 1985. Short, real-life situations that force young people to make difficult choices between conflicting values.

Maslow, Abraham. *Motivation and Personality.* New York: Harper and Row, 1970. The classic work on motivation and the basic drive to meet certain needs in priority order.

McDonough, Reginald M. *Working with Volunteer Leaders in the Church.* Nashville: Broadman, 1976. Equipping volunteers who will in turn equip others.

McGinnis, Alan Loy. *Bringing Out the Best in People.* Minneapolis: Augsburg, 1985. A motivational tool to help in the recruiting and encouraging of team members in your ministry.

New Roles for Youth in School and Community. New York: Citation Press, 1974. Suggests many ways to use youths as volunteer workers; a helpful resource for channeling the motivated student.

Peters, Tom, and Nancy Austin. *A Passion for Excellence.* New York: Random House, 1985. This sequel to *In Search of Excellence* explores what goes into the making of an excellent leader.

Reichter, Arlo. *The Group Retreat Book.* Loveland, Colo.: Group Books, 1984. A how-to guide for designing retreats, including thirty-four ready-to-use retreat designs for junior or senior highers.

Rice, Wayne, ed. *Ideas.* El Cajon, Calif.: Youth Specialties, 1968 to 1991. Hundreds of ideas in forty-nine volumes (so far) for youth group meetings, holidays, special events, fund-raisers, games, publicity, and worship.

Rice, Wayne. *Up Close and Personal: How to Build Community in Your Youth Group.* Grand Rapids: YS/Zondervan, 1989.

Robbins, Duffy. *Programming to Build Disciples.* Wheaton, Ill.: Victor, 1987. A practical manual for turning a vision of discipling young people into a usable program.

Sanders, J. Oswald. *Spiritual Leadership.* Chicago: Moody Press, 1979. One of the most sought-after books on the individual life and character of the teacher/leader.

Schaller, Lyle. *Activating the Passive Church.* Nashville: Abingdon, 1981. Instructions on motivating the apathetic members in the church. The principles are somewhat transferable to work with youth.

Senter, Mark. *The Art of Recruiting Volunteers.* Wheaton, Ill.: Victor, 1983. Assembling a team ministry in a local church setting? This manual is complete with sample handouts, recruiting calendars, and evaluation tools.

Shawchuck, Norman. *How to Be a More Effective Church Leader.* Downers Grove, Ill.: Spiritual Growth Resources, 1981. Good pointers for the leader on how to improve relationships with peers in leadership as well as with those who are served.

Smith, Fred. *Learning to Lead.* Waco, Tex.: Word, 1986. Observations from a veteran on the way we learn to assume responsibility for guiding the efforts of others.

Stone, J. David, and Rose Mary Miller. *Volunteer Youth Workers.* Loveland, Colo.: Group Books, 1985. Basic information for team ministry, including sample job descriptions, recruiting letters, and ideas for involving parents in the youth leadership team.

Strommen, Merton. *Five Cries of Youth.* New York: Harper and Row, 1974.

Volunteering: A Manual for Students. The National Student Volunteer Program, VISTA, Washington, D.C. A manual designed to channel the energies of the motivated young person or youth group.

Warren, Michael. *Youth and the Future of the Church.* New York: Seabury, 1982. Evaluates the ways we can build young people for future leadership.

Wilson, Marlene. *The Effective Management of Voluntary Programs.* Boulder, Colo.: Volunteer Management Association, 1976. A recommended work on the placement of volunteers based on effectiveness and abilities, rather than need and urgency.

Resource Organizations: Agencies for Training in Service and Leadership

Camfel Productions. 136 North Olive Avenue, Monrovia, CA 91016. Top-of-the-line producers of Christian multi-image productions for use in youth rallies, school assemblies, and other outreach events.

Compassion International. P.O. Box 7000, Colorado Springs, CO 80933. Offers the Compassion Project to youth groups as a tool for educating students and getting them involved in helping the poor.

Group, Incorporated. Box 481, Loveland, CO 80539. In addition to publishing magazines and books, Group, Inc. also sponsors major events for youth groups and youth leaders, including the National Christian Youth Congress, *Group* Magazine Workcamps, and the Youth Ministry University.

Habitat for Humanity. 419 West Church Street, Americus, GA 31709. Builds homes for the disadvantaged around the world. Teenagers can go as work teams.

InterVarsity Christian Fellowship. P.O. Box 7895, Madison, WI 53707. Sponsors Urbana missions conventions for high school seniors and older. Held every three years.

National Institute of Youth Ministry. 24422 Del Prado, Suite 12, Dana Point, CA 92629. Sponsors a variety of seminars and training events for youth workers as well as the Handling Your Hormones seminar for adolescents.

Paragon Productions. Campus Crusade for Christ International, Arrowhead Springs, #86-00, San Bernardino, CA 92414. Media producers for outreach programs in high schools, colleges, and churches.

Servant Events. Board of Youth Ministries, Lutheran Church—Missouri Synod, 1333 South Kirkwood, St. Louis, MO 63122. Sponsors workcamp opportunities for kids and adults.

Sierra Treks: Wilderness Trips by Trek, Inc. 15097 Greensprings Highway, Ashland, OR 97520. Wilderness experiences for youth groups in Washington, Oregon, and California that use stress camping to foster Christian growth.

Teen Missions International. Box 1056, Merritt Island, FL 32952. The experts on teenage work teams, TMI sends thousands of them from across the U.S. to work experiences around the world.

Youth for Christ. Box 419, Wheaton, IL 60189. Planners of the D.C. '88 high-schoolers' conference.

Youth Specialties Ministries. 1224 Greenfield Drive, El Cajon, CA 92021. Longtime youth ministry experts sponsor a variety of seminars and conferences for youth (Grow For It and Riptide '88), youth workers (National Youth Workers Convention and National Resource Seminar for Youth Workers), and parents of teenagers (Understanding Your Teenager).

Student Study Sheets

MAKING A WORLD OF DIFFERENCE IN A WORLD OF NEED

(For Week 2)
Making an Impact by Learning to Care

A sign in a southern California relief agency, World Vision, is a prayer that reads: *"Lord, let my heart be broken by the things that break the heart of God."*

We need a generation of teenagers that learn to pray like that. Recent research[1] tells us that in the next thirty minutes

   29 kids will attempt suicide

   57 will run away from home

   14 teenage girls will give birth to illegitimate babies

   22 teenage girls will get an abortion

 685 teenagers will take some form of narcotics

 188 will experience a serious drinking problem

 285 teenagers will become victims of broken homes

 228 kids will be beaten, molested, or abused by their parents

The facts are staggering and the real fact is this: The call of Christ is the call to care! Take some time to read the following verses and write what you think each has to say about people who are hurting, about hunger, about poverty, and about caring.

Matthew 25:34–40	
Acts 2:44–45	
Acts 11:27–30	
Romans 12:13	

1. Rich van Pelt, "How to Help Your Friends in Trouble," Grow For It Tour, 1989.

Which of the following would you be most excited about doing in order to make an impact? Fill in each of the blanks with a number ranking them from one (most concerned) to eight (least concerned).

_____ Pray for victims of hunger and poverty.

_____ Pray for people at my school who seem to be struggling.

_____ Support a child with Compassion International or another relief agency.

_____ Investigate the possibility of our youth group taking a missions trip.

_____ Look into our youth group going into the city to learn about the needs there.

_____ Meet with young people at the local juvenile hall.

_____ Talk as a youth group about a project we could do to alleviate world hunger.

_____ Help plan a local service project in our own community.

Now, here's where the fun starts. Pick one of the above ideas that you rated the highest and write in the box below a specific action plan to make it happen.

Action Plan

Optional Project

Most American teenagers have more stuff than 98 percent of the rest of the world. The following is a great way to balance the scales. Do a little scavenger hunt to figure out how much stuff you have, then figure out how much you owe for each of the following:

_____ Ten cents for each pair of shoes you have (five cents extra for each pair of Air Jordans)

_____ Twenty-five cents for every movie you have seen in the last month

_____ Ten cents for every TV in your house

_____ Fifty cents if you have a TV in your room

_____ Fifteen cents for every VCR in your house

_____ Fifty cents if you own your own stereo system (twenty-five cents more if you have a CD system)

_____ Ten cents for every car your family has

_____ Twenty-five cents if you have your own car

_____ Twenty-five cents for every watch you own

_____ Seventy-five cents if you have a job or get an allowance

_____ Twenty-five cents if you have ever called Domino's and ordered a pizza

_____ Ten cents for each album or CD you own

_____ TOTAL AMOUNT

Total it up. Collect the money and contact a good relief agency where you can send the money. Send it in and pray that God will use the money to make an impact.

"... whatever you did for
one of the least of these ...
you did for me." *Matthew 25:40*

MAKING A WORLD OF DIFFERENCE IN A WORLD OF NEED

(For Week 3)
Learning to Lead by Learning to Serve

The church would be in real trouble if everyone exercised only the gifts that brought attention to themselves. Leonard Bernstein, the famous orchestra conductor, was asked "What is the most difficult instrument to play?" He responded: "Second fiddle. I can get plenty of first violinists, but to find one who plays *second* violin with as much enthusiasm or *second* French horn or *second* flute, now that's a problem. And yet if no one plays second, we have no harmony."[1]

Read the following verses and answer the questions.

Read Mark 10:45
What does this verse say about Jesus' purpose in coming?

What effect would it have on your life in you lived with the same goal in mind?

Read Philippians 2:1–9
What do these verses say about living a life of service?

How did Jesus model that kind of life?

Read John 13:1–20
Why did Jesus wash the disciples' feet?

1. Charles R. Swindoll, *Improving Your Serve* (Waco, Tex.: Word, 1981), 34.

SERVICE SURVEY

On a scale of one to ten, rate your responses to the following statements:

1	2	3	4	5	6	7	8	9	10
NO		RARELY		MAYBE		SOMETIMES			YES!

I enjoy meeting the needs of others. _____

You'll frequently find me volunteering my time to help with the needs of the church. _____

I'm the type of person who likes to reach out to the less fortunate. _____

I feel good when I help with the routine jobs at the church. _____

You'll often find me volunteering to do "behind the scenes" activities that few notice, but that must be done. _____

I clean up after a meeting without being asked. _____

I seldom think twice before doing a task that might not bring me praise. _____

I receive joy doing jobs that others see as "thankless." _____

I am able to do jobs that others won't do. _____

In the box below write one or two ideas from the above list that are ways in which you would like to serve. Write one practical way you would do each one.

```



```

OVERTIME: Name a friend who has "washed your feet" (that is, served and helped you in some way). Take a minute and write them a note of encouragement.

Source: Jim Burns and Doug Fields, *Congratulations! You Are Gifted!* (Eugene, Ore.: Harvest House, 1986).

MAKING A WORLD OF DIFFERENCE IN A WORLD OF NEED

(For Week 4)
Discovering Your Spiritual Gifts
OR
Me—Gifted? You've Got to Be Kidding!

Hard as it is to believe, the Bible makes it clear that we are gifted. This Study Sheet is designed to enable you to discover what the Bible says about being gifted and how to discover what your gifts are! There may be times when you do not feel very gifted, but the fact is that, as a Christian, you have received spiritual gifts designed especially for you by God.

A spiritual gift is a special ability God gives Christians to use in service for God's glory and purpose.

There are four main sections in the New Testament that let us in on what spiritual gifts are all about. Read each passage of Scripture and list the various gifts under each section.

Romans 12:6–8
1.
2.
3.
4.
5.
6.
7.

1 Corinthians 12:4–11; 28–30
1.
2.
3.
4.
5.
6.
7.
8.
9.
10.
11.
12.

Ephesians 4:7, 8, 11, 12
1.
2.
3.
4.
5.

1 Peter 4:9–11
1.
2.
3.

These passages make two things clear:

    1. There are no *ungifted* Christians (you are needed).

    2. No one person has *all* the gifts (we need each other).

Read 1 Corinthians 12:1. What does it say about being uninformed?

_____

_____

_____

Read 1 Peter 4:10 and rewrite the verse in your own words.

_____

_____

_____

There are three great benefits to discovering and using your spiritual gifts.

    1. Knowing your spiritual gifts gives you confidence.

    2. Discovering your spiritual gifts gives you direction.

    3. Using your spiritual gifts gives you purpose.

Looking at the spiritual gifts list you have written on the previous page, write down the three that you think are most likely gifts you have. If you are having a hard time, call a friend or someone who knows you well and ask them. It's a great way to get positive affirmation. Then write a short explanation of how you exercise each gift.

Gift: Explanation:	Gift: Explanation:	Gift: Explanation:

1 Peter 4:10 tells us to use our gifts in serving one another. Let's get practical. Take a couple of minutes and list three people that you could serve and one practical way you will serve each person this week. Possibilities include: serving your parents, friends, youth worker, pastor, teachers, brothers or sisters, grandparents.

Person	Practical Service Project
Person	Practical Service Project
Person	Practical Service Project

171

MAKING A WORLD OF DIFFERENCE IN A WORLD OF NEED

(For Week 5)
Developing Your Spiritual Gifts by Learning to Encourage

People in general and teenagers in particular need encouragement! Today's student knows that the average campus is a self-image war zone. A good friend of mine had this written in his annual.

"God Created Rivers,
God Created Lakes,
God Created You, Jim.
Everyone Makes Mistakes."

Unfortunately, for many teenagers, that is all the feedback they ever hear. As Christian leaders, one of the ministries we are called to is the ministry of encouragement. For the next week, read one of the following Scriptures each day. Answer the questions in each column and take the encouragement action step. You will be amazed at how God will use you because, for most of the people in your life, a little encouragement will go a long way!

DAY	SCRIPTURE	STUDY QUESTION	ACTION STEP
Monday	*Romans 12:9–21*	What commands are given in this passage?	Pick the verse that compels you most from this section. Write it here. Write one specific step you can take to obey this command.
Tuesday	*Galatians 6:1–10*	What does this passage say about our friendships?	Write and send a note to an adult in your church who has encouraged you.

DAY	SCRIPTURE	STUDY QUESTION	ACTION STEP
Wednesday	*1 Corinthians 13*	Make a list of the characteristics of a loving person found in this passage.	Circle the one quality that you would most like to have describe you. Pray that God will develop that in your life.
Thursday	*Acts 4:36–37; 9:26–27; 15:36–40*	What was Barnabas's nickname? List all the ways that he encouraged others.	List a person here who has been an encouragement to you. Call that person and say thanks.
Friday	*Mark 2:1–12*	How did the four friends encourage their friend? What obstacles did they have to overcome?	Write the names of three friends you would like to bring to Jesus. 1. 2. 3. Take a minute and pray for a way to encourage each of these friends.

Discover Your Spiritual Gifts!
(Teen Edition)

DISCOVER YOUR SPIRITUAL GIFTS! (Teen Edition)

(For Week 5)

Instructions: For each question, enter the number that most applies to you.

3 = THAT'S ME!
2 = This is PROBABLY me.
1 = This is PROBABLY NOT me.
0 = DEFINITELY NOT me!

_____ 1. I try to worry more about the needs of others than my own.

_____ 2. People come to me when they need to talk out a problem.

_____ 3. I would like to give money to those in need.

_____ 4. I enjoy explaining the Bible to others.

_____ 5. I like to try to help others know God better.

_____ 6. I don't mind being seen with people who aren't that popular.

_____ 7. When I see needy people on cold nights, I really feel like inviting them to my home.

_____ 8. On Friday nights, I am usually the one who decides where we go and what we do.

_____ 9. I like to tell others about my relationship with God.

_____ 10. I have confidence that God will get me through both good and bad times.

_____ 11. I like doing jobs that most people don't want to do.

_____ 12. I am known for my positive attitude.

_____ 13. I get a real kick out of giving stuff away.

_____ 14. I like studying the Bible so I can explain it to others.

_____ 15. I like to pray for and with others.

_____ 16. I would like to work with disabled people.

_____ 17. I like having friends stay overnight at my house.

_____ 18. I like to organize and motivate groups of people.

_____ 19. I can sometimes make discussions relate to God.

_____ 20. I believe that God can do things that seem impossible.

_____ 21. I have helped other people so their work was easier.

_____ 22. I like to help sad people feel better.

_____ 23. I try to be smart with my money so that I can give extra money to people who need it.

_____ 24. I like learning and studying the Bible.

_____ 25. I would love to lead a Bible study at school.

_____ 26. I feel very sympathetic toward the needy.

_____ 27. I don't feel disrupted when there are guests at my home.

_____ 28. I have encouraged others to finish a job.

_____ 29. I would like to help someone else become a Christian.

_____ 30. I have confidence that God will keep his promises even when things are bad.

_____ 31. I don't mind doing little jobs that other people don't consider important.

_____ 32. I can encourage others through what I say.

_____ 33. I know that God will meet my needs, so I want to give freely to others.

_____ 34. I could show others what different ideas in the Bible mean.

_____ 35. I like to serve people to show that God cares for them.

_____ 36. If a friend is sick, I call to see how he/she is doing.

_____ 37. I like having company come to my house.

_____ 38. I would like to lead, inspire, and motivate people to do God's work.

_____ 39. I would like to tell others that Jesus is the Savior and help them see the positive results.

_____ 40. I trust that I can call on God and know that he will be there when "impossible" situations happen.

_____ 41. Sometimes when I do jobs, nobody notices, but I don't mind.

_____ 42. I like it when people are happier after I have talked to them.

_____ 43. I have given away my money or belongings to those in need.

_____ 44. I think that I could show others how to find answers on their own.

_____ 45. I would like to help bring people back to Christ who have wandered away from him.

_____ 46. When I see a homeless person, I really want to help.

_____ 47. My friends come over to my house because they feel comfortable there.

_____ 48. When I'm in a group, sometimes people look to me to take charge.

_____ 49. I take any opportunity I can to tell people about Christ.

_____ 50. When everything looks bad, I can still trust God.

Spiritual Gifts Test

Tabulation

Instructions:

1. Put your response (0 to 3) to each test question in the blank next to the appropriate number on the chart below.

2. Add up the numbers going across the blanks and record them in the box under "TOTAL."

					TOTAL	GIFT
						A
1 ___	11 ___	21 ___	31 ___	41 ___		
						B
2 ___	12 ___	22 ___	32 ___	42 ___		
						C
3 ___	13 ___	23 ___	33 ___	43 ___		
						D
4 ___	14 ___	24 ___	34 ___	44 ___		
						E
5 ___	15 ___	25 ___	35 ___	45 ___		
						F
6 ___	16 ___	26 ___	36 ___	46 ___		
						G
7 ___	17 ___	27 ___	37 ___	47 ___		
						H
8 ___	18 ___	28 ___	38 ___	48 ___		
						I
9 ___	19 ___	29 ___	39 ___	49 ___		
						J
10 ___	20 ___	30 ___	40 ___	50 ___		

Explanation

GIFT A: *Helping.* The ability to assist and serve other people.

GIFT B: *Encouraging.* The ability to support people and help them to regain hope.

GIFT C: *Giving.* The ability to give your time and money so that it can be used for God's work.

GIFT D: *Teaching.* The ability to teach the Bible in such a way that people learn and grow.

GIFT E: *Pastoring.* The ability to effectively guide and care for people in their walk with God.

GIFT F: *Mercy.* The ability to act out of compassion toward those who are suffering.

GIFT G: *Hospitality.* The gift of being friendly and generous to guests.

GIFT H: *Leading.* The ability to motivate others to use their spiritual gifts and to do their best for the work of the Lord.

GIFT I: *Evangelism.* The ability to help others to come to know Jesus personally.

GIFT J: *Faith.* The ability to have a confident belief that God will always do what is the very best.

Assessment

Determine your demonstrated, probable spiritual gift(s) as follows: If the score in the "TOTAL" section is

12–15: There is great evidence that God has blessed you with this spiritual gift.

8–11: There is a strong possibility that God has blessed you with this spiritual gift.

4–7: There is a good possibility that God could be developing this gift in you.

0–4: You are spiritually gifted, probably in an area other than this one.